The Later Dater

Valerie Gibson

Table of Contents

Foreword

Foreword

The idea for *The Later Dater: A Guide for the Newly Single Woman Over 50*, was a natural progression from my last book *Cougar: A Guide for Older Women Dating Younger Men*, published in 2002.

Having launched the cougar trend with my book, first in Canada and then in the United States, I was astonished, and gratified, to see it not only become an worldwide trend but also that *cougar*, as applied to strong, independent, sexy older women dating younger men, became an accepted and recognizable descriptive word.

Along the way, the term has had wildly varying lives and interpretations. Some were flattering and supportive, but many were insensitive and derogatory because the populace and media often misunderstood, either unwittingly or deliberately, what being a "cougar" really meant.

Cougar evoked a strong and powerful image of the new older women of the millennium — sexy, sophisticated, successful, and independent women over 40 — who not only preferred to date younger men but did not want to marry, co-habit, or have children.

Cougars deliberately look for short-term liaisons with younger men who suit their energy level, hectic lifestyle, and career aspirations and meet their sexual needs. Although cougars sometimes form rewarding connections, rarely do their encounters become serious, long-term relationships.

The fundamental difference between a cougar and any other single older woman who happens to be dating younger is that cougars are always in control of the relationship, both sexually and emotionally (and often even financially), deciding what will happen when and for how long. It's the sexual control that appears to have rocked the boat of societal approval since the introduction of the trend.

For centuries, the male partner always held the reins of mating relationships. He chose the partner and decided how the relationship would progress, when and how sex would be initiated, and when and how the relationship would end. Handing women control in a romantic or sexual relationship was completely unnatural and something to fear.

Strong, powerful, intelligent, and sexual older women have always been treated with suspicion by society, especially if single. Then along came Boomer women. Brave, questioning, educated, intelligent, active, and aware, they were not willing, like women of previous generations, to accept the ancient and traditional dictates of who they were, who they should be, or how they should behave. What's more, they absolutely refused to believe that they should fade into the background just because they were getting older. They were also not willing to accept that their sexuality would suddenly disappear, never to return. (And, hey, if it did, they'd obviously do something about it.)

Many Boomer women found that, far from being the touted, feared abyss of decay, deterioration, disease, and despair, getting older was a fascinating adventure, full of promise and excitement and, yes, sexuality. It was in fact new and untrodden territory, open to exploration and experimentation.

This was a revelation for many older women, especially because increasingly large numbers of them, Boomers and beyond, were becoming footloose and fancy-free in mid and late life. Far from allowing themselves to be pushed aside and discarded as in generations past, older women were deciding to stand up and be counted. They realized that they not only had options that didn't exist in generations past, but that they had many valuable assets and abilities to exercise and many active, fulfilling years ahead in which to use and enjoy them.

Many single older women also decided they'd like to share the journey with someone new — in other words, find a new relationship and perhaps a partner.

But if the new world of aging is virgin territory, so to speak, then venturing into the dating arena to find someone can be more than just unfamiliar at this stage of life — it can be scary, unsettling, and a minefield of mistakes, which means a single older woman might simply give up and refuse to date for fear of the emotional cost. And that's a great pity because a good relationship is enormously beneficial to our health, emotional wellbeing, and longevity.

So the idea for this book was born — a book that would give cheerful advice and help to single, female Boomers and beyond on navigating and enjoying the dating world of today. Rather than focus on women who prefer younger men, the book reaches out to single women of 50, 60, 70, and above who want to date older, same age, or younger men and who need either a nudge in the right direction or some help understanding the intricacies, pleasures, pitfalls, and rules of what can be a complex world of relationships.

I hope *The Later Dater* informs and helps you.

Introduction

Introduction

Today's single older woman is hot!

What's more she doesn't want to be categorized by her age and she doesn't want to be called a senior, pensioner, granny (even if she is one), or any other trendy name touted by marketers to make money from the growing demographic.

She's the new older woman (NOW), and she's sexy, smart, vital, successful, and desirable!

Most people personally know several single women like this who, despite wanting to find someone to share their lifestyle, don't have or can't find a partner or a relationship.

Yet they're attractive to men in a wide range of ages, so why aren't more of them actively dating and finding new relationships?

"It's demeaning," "All the good men are taken," "They're all too old," "I wouldn't know what to do anymore," All they want is sex," "My family would be horrified," and "I don't want to give up my space or freedom," are just a few of the many excuses from many attractive single older women who, although they state firmly they're not lonely and lead active, busy, fulfilled lives, nevertheless would like to have another relationship or companionship at this interesting time of their lives.

Yet today's older dating scene is often daunting and fills older women with dread. Some see it as unknown territory filled with quicksand. Yet to others who have tried it, while they agree it can be an emotional roller coaster at times, it can also be great fun, interesting, exciting, and eventually fulfilling and worthwhile.

But it's a fact that dating for the 50-plus single woman is a relatively new social phenomenon. It didn't exist, or at least wasn't acceptable, until recent years. As a result, the 50-plus single woman who is ready and willing to actively look for a relationship is a relatively new phenomenon as well.

Until recent times, such women were led to believe they were irrelevant to society, lacking in value, and undesirable — certainly not sexy or sensual, and generally not wanted as new partners by men. Discarded or pushed aside and expected to take their traditional position as mothers, grandmothers, aunts, parental and child caregivers, and spinsters of the parish, they often felt invisible.

In past decades, if they were unfortunate enough to become widows, they were not only sometimes made to wear mourning black for the rest of their lives, but society frowned upon their remarriage. Eternal widowhood was often their lot in life. If the rare remarriage did occur, it was mostly because of connections within their family circle and was, for many women, often not with someone of their choice.

Centuries ago, strong, single older women were feared and seen as a troubling factor in the scheme of the normal progression of life and the control of the populace. Women at that point also generally died before men because medical help for women until past Victorian times was cursory, ignorant, often experimental, and frequently ineffective.

And, if they dared to step outside the bounds of general society's rules, or were singularly independent, intelligent, knowledgeable, or even attractive, they were often shunned or repressed. In past centuries, they were sometimes even accused of being witches.

Then there are centuries of procreative indoctrination. Older women were led to believe that menopause was the end of their usefulness because they could no longer provide progeny. They were also told that after menopause, their sexuality would vanish almost overnight and with it their natural desire and, especially, their desirability.

Only in recent decades have women begun to realize they have been sold a twisted bill of goods and, possibly, a controlling fabrication.

Many women discovered that their sexuality, far from disappearing overnight, as they'd been told, surged gloriously as they aged, which made them confused, anxious, and afraid that something was wrong with them. Many found that even if their libido dipped from time to time, it resolutely remained with them into old age.

And medically speaking, there is no reason that women, give or take limitations of health and ability, can't feel sexual, and desire and enjoy sexual activity the same way that men do throughout their lives.

These days, if there is any hormonal flagging of the libido (a major reason for a woman's lack of sexual interest), it's relatively easily nudged back into place for those determined to retain their sexuality. Drugs or natural remedies and methods allow women to balance the drop in hormonal activity that often accompanies menopause.

That mid-life drop in a woman's libido can also be psychological, for some women believe that they should not have sexual feelings and desires and therefore deny and repress them. Perhaps a long-term passionless marriage or poor sexual activity with a current partner has led to the slow death of a woman's natural sexuality.

But thanks to education, awareness, and the prodded progress of female medicine, knowledge, awareness, and attitudes are changing gloriously.

Welcome to the new world of fabulous aging, where women are coming to grips with the fact that mid and late life can actually be an exciting adventure and that being single in mid and late life means new choices, options, and moving forward with confidence and joie de vivre.

Women of 50 and upwards now form a major part of the biggest growing demographic of our day and of the future: the mid and late life single. They may be single after a long-term marriage or relationship — or several shorter-term ones — or may have remained single by choice, having chosen instead to concentrate on a career, a business, or other responsibilities. They may have also decided to re-examine their sexual preferences and orientation.

In addition to increased awareness of the benefits of diet and exercise, the new longevity has helped change the future view of aging. Nowadays it's entirely possible that a 50-year-old woman (who has a longer life expectancy than a man) may have another 40-plus years to live. In fact, the human lifespan has increased so much that many more people, both male and female, will now live to 90 or even 100.

It's undoubtedly true that few people want to "date" at those advanced ages, but it's remarkable and exciting just how many single older people are now looking for a relationship at the ages of 50, 60, 70 and, yes, even 80.

They're fitter and more sophisticated and educated than any previous generation and, far from thinking life drops into an abyss at the age of 50, many of them feel that they're at the start of a wonderful new period of their lives. Often, they would like to share this journey with another partner.

Yet, particularly for women over 50, dating is a strange and fearful step. Many cite the fact that, particularly in large towns or cities, there are more women than men in the older single age groups and also point out that, statistically, only a very small pool of compatible men is available to them.

Discounting those men who are married, attached, gay, addicted, ill, or only looking for a much younger woman, plus adding healthy and reasonably fit as requirements, and the numbers reduce even further. While this has led an increasing number of older women to expand their partnership options and consider younger men as well, and, they are, after all, only following in the footsteps of centuries of men who have dated and married younger women, the majority of 50-and-beyond women aren't looking for a younger "hottie." They want someone closer to their age they feel they can relate to, share life with, and who has had, and is having, similar life experiences. And if family, church, club, friends, or work networks fail or are unavailable, this means getting into the dating arena.

But dating has changed since they were younger. Everything is different, from an older woman's list of requirements, to male attitudes, to social skills, sexual etiquette, diseases, and, especially, the modern methods of meeting each other such as through social media and technology. Even how a relationship is conducted at a much later age is different in today's environment, with personal needs, dreams, and desires changing as one ages. As a result, many 50-plus women draw back from such unknown territory when dating is suggested or presented as the way to meet the single opposite sex.

For them, there is no template for what is a relatively new and untried social activity for this age group. And often a major concern is the familial reaction and social stigma placed on older, single women if they are sexually active, especially after the death of a spouse. Which is such a pity. A romantic relationship is very beneficial to a human's wellbeing, and when older people are part of such a union, they're happier and healthier and live longer than those who remain resolutely single.

These are great incentives to get out into the dating world and find someone. It can truly open up your world and make mid and late life the most exciting and interesting part of your life journey yet!

The Later Dater will help you confidently navigate and enjoy the dating world of today while maintaining your self-esteem.

Chapter One

Starting Out

No matter what their age, finding the "ideal" partner looms large in the head of single women, and often in their imagination. Despite changing the requirements somewhat over the years, women rarely let go of their romantic dream.

Often based, if unconsciously, on actors, fantasy figures or situations in novels, movies or television shows, we may believe that one day, the "man of our dreams" will walk right into our life and that will be "it." Many of us find this a tough fantasy to give up, and it can continue throughout our lives, despite the fact that we've no doubt had plenty of experience with relationship realism by the time we become a later dater.

It's true that Mr. Right may appear suddenly for some. But such appearances are few and, in truth, he may turn out to not quite the man of their dreams.

It happened to me once.

I was late in getting ready to rush out to a new date and there was a knock on my door. Annoyed and flustered, I rushed down to open the door. My mouth dropped when I pulled it open.

There stood an extremely attractive, sexy man, a real estate agent I knew slightly, holding a copy of my cougar book and asking if I could sign it for his friend.

Despite being late for my date, I invited him in and signed his book.

When he was leaving, he kissed me on the cheek as a thank you, and my knees almost buckled. Later on, when I returned from my date, I found a bottle of wine and a note with his cell phone number on my doorstep.

I couldn't resist. It was the start of a long, very passionate relationship that I thought would go on forever. (Hey, as I said, we're all hopeful romantics at heart.)

Yes, he was my dream man — handsome, articulate, sexy, intelligent, fun, and spontaneous. But when reality set in and I realized he knew only too well that he was every other woman's dream man as well, I came off cloud nine and major issues emerged.

I became painfully aware I was yet another besotted woman in his life, and the feeling wasn't reciprocated. More to the point, I was the most conveniently available, because I worked from home. That was all there was: home visits. Not quite my "dream."

Although it was painful when it ended (probably because I felt more than foolish at ignoring the obvious) I look back and don't think dark thoughts. Well, maybe only one or two. What I do think is, wow! I had a marvelous time with him, and I wouldn't have missed any of it. And, yes, that does make me feel better about my own decisions, obviously.

Like so many women with an "ideal" still in my head despite my life experiences, I was swept off my feet into an illusion and blinded to reality by someone who fit the description. But, in my defence, how often does a gorgeous man knock on your front door? Rarely or never, except in novels, movies, or television shows.

But going out into the dating world with a list of requirements that describe your "ideal" partner and being determined to stick to it until he's found, is a good way to sabotage your best efforts from the start. By the time you've reached the joyous mid or late part of your life, you know what you want — and don't want — in a partner.

For most later daters, the person they're looking for is probably totally unlike the one, or ones, from their past who may have betrayed or hurt them. Or, conversely, maybe the later dater is looking for a partner who most resembles a former beloved.

The best advice I have for every later dater is this: DITCH THE LIST. Also ditch the ideals, the fantasies, and the wish to clone anyone. They will just hold you back from what might be a completely new and exhilarating experience.

With the new (to you) territory of dating will come a completely fresh array of men who not only are all shapes, sizes, levels of financial security, outlooks, habits, needs, desires, and attitudes, but who will also be new experiences. Of course, they may also arrive with their own list of "requirements." But more on that later.

So while short, overweight, and hairy men, for instance, might not be your idea of a perfect partner, by overlooking the men that don't fit your "list" you may miss out on a kind, funny, generous, loving man who will adore you and is wonderful in bed.

If a tall, handsome, rich, successful man tops your list, join the club. Such men, especially if older, top the lists of many female daters of all ages. And with there being more single women than men in the later dater category, these men are well aware of their market value and scarcity. All they have to do is just be there.

Obviously with all the attention they get (and at times it can seem like a shark-feeding frenzy) the competition will not only be fierce but often impenetrable for the average woman. So it makes good sense to consider all types and personalities in order to discover that special gem of a man.

But other than ditching the requirement list, what other preparations should a later dater make in order to be ready for the dating arena?

Updating yourself

Updating your image will boost your confidence and self-esteem. Maybe you're still dressing in styles that have long gone out of fashion or are looking tired. Take a good look at your wardrobe, including footwear, and understand that clothing to wear for dating and meeting men can be quite different from the clothing you wear to work, at home, or to the grocery store. Whatever you wear should flatter you and enhance your best points. Perhaps your makeup and hairstyle could benefit from a new look; maybe you also need to finally start that diet and fitness regime. Even buying some pretty (or hot) underwear can give you a sense of an exciting new start.

Although the idea may sound superficial, going out into the dating world requires packaging the goods, so to speak, and smart marketing.

Looking for a new relationship, especially in mid and late life, is a highly competitive field. It is, in fact, much like searching for a special job, planning a vacation, or starting a business. It takes time, effort, smarts, some research and, in the hunt for a partner, presenting yourself in your best light.

You may feel strongly that, at this time of your life, whoever you meet has to accept you as you are and, because you're intelligent, articulate, and great company, that should be enough for them. And, of course, basically, you're right.

But we live in a world where image is everything, and the first impression is a lasting one, whether we like it or not. It's said that people evaluate you in three seconds when they first meet you, so if you want to find a relationship, present the best of yourself.

Health and fitness

By this time of our life, we're only too aware of how our body works and, particularly, how it looks. We may not be totally happy with our physical image, but time and knowledge has also given us the ability to know how to make the best of what we have and how to change what we dislike, if we want to. We also understand how aging affects us. After all, we're going through it aren't we?

But most of all, we've learned exactly what generations before us knew only too well and perhaps bored us with when we were young: that good health is the key to aging well and happily.

Over the years, medical knowledge about health, fitness, and their effect on the aging process has not only improved but has increased by leaps and bounds. We're come through the eras of sparse knowledge and, often, even sparser attention, about women's health and aging.

But at times, it seems like it has gone the other way, with endless attention and publicity about the diseases and ailments we may face as we age. "Disease of the month" fixation I call it, which doesn't help, in my opinion, to allay the ingrained fears and dread so many women have about getting older. The truth is, aging can be quite fascinating, fulfilling, and exciting for older women, in a number of ways, with many actually enjoying good health.

Many women say the biggest concern facing them when they want to date again is their weight. Usually they think they have a little too much of it. While it's true we live in a world that worships thinness in women (we don't seem to have the same concern about men), studies have shown that having a little extra weight when older can be beneficial to health and longevity. And health experts state it's often not weight that matters, but whether or not the woman is healthy. Mind you, it has to be *moderately* extra weight.

So, as much as women may sigh about what they see as too simplistic, the answer to maintaining a healthy weight (and body) has never changed: a healthy diet and regular exercise. Experts agree that staying active is key. That doesn't mean endless hours at the gym. Who has the time these days for such dedication? It's *continuous* moderate activity during a week that provides the most benefit to the heart and lungs, reducing the likelihood of a heart attack and lowering blood pressure. It also helps improve self-esteem and mental health and relieve depression, three problem areas that can beset aging women.

Now, most busy women of today would say they are actually in perpetual motion, which is undoubtedly true, but many may be in sedentary jobs at a computer, for instance, or are not motivated to add "keeping active and fit" to their schedule. Yet the benefits of regular moderate exercise to health such as swimming, gardening, yoga, cycling, or dancing are enormous and surely far outweigh the effort and schedule interruption.

Sex

There's no question that one of the most enjoyable exercises, at any age, is sex. It keeps you flexible and helps circulation and heart activity, which nourishes your skin and complexion to give you that youthful "glow." And, best of all, it makes you happy and feel good.

And if this area of enjoyment has been lacking in your life, an upcoming chapter will refresh your memory and give you some tips on dealing with sex later in life.

Diet

We've been overwhelmed for decades by diet information: what's good for us and bad for us, and what will put weight on, take it off, put us at risk for health problems, help us live longer, or shorten our lives.

Most women, therefore, know about the benefits of fresh fruit and vegetables, fish and lean meat, legumes, and whole grain breads. Avoiding or limiting high fat food, smoked meats, salt, and animal fats (butter, whole milk, cheese) while keeping your consumption of sugar to as little as you can, is a big step towards healthy eating, as is cutting down on snacks, cookies, and cakes. We also know to read labels on the groceries we buy, especially processed foods.

As much as most of us love a glass of wine or two, and studies say a glass of red wine a day can be beneficial, be aware that all alcohol adds calories to your diet. The calories increase if it's a "mixed" drink such as a gin and tonic.

Boomers and beyond are fortunate to live in an era when there is advanced medical help available should any problem occur, but a great deal of being fit and healthy in later life really depends on ourselves. Getting regular screening and testing for teeth, bones, breasts, heart, lungs, eyes, ears, and joints can lead to early detection of problems and fast remedy, if needed.

I know it seems as though the list of lifestyle changes or additions for having a healthy mid and late life appear somewhat onerous, yet the aim of this chapter is help prepare women who want to try dating to move forward with self-confidence and optimism.

And if you think the onus is just on women, it's not. It works both ways. Men also need to present themselves as best they can in order to impress you. Most later daters understand the concept of "mutual."

Emotional readiness

But preparing yourself emotionally is perhaps the most important part of getting back into the dating world, particularly if it's happening after a long stretch of time when you were either in a relationship or a single.

And although this sounds simplistic, it means understanding that the first man you meet and date will not necessarily be Mr. Right (although this can happen, but rarely!). You need to meet a number of different men to find out for sure what type and personality you want to share your time, emotions, intimacy, and life experiences with.

It will also mean that among the varied, interesting, and sometimes exciting encounters there will inevitably be some disappointment, disillusion, and depressing moments. Meet the average dating scenario.

A high degree of positive optimism — and tolerance — is therefore essential in the later dater's world. And just like with any relationship search at any age, you may find someone you think is Mr. Perfect but he, sadly, doesn't see you as Miss Perfect-for-him (and vice versa). If it isn't the right relationship for you, accept it and move on. Besides, you're far too sensible and experienced to become a stalker... A realistic attitude and a stalwart sense of humour will get you through many situations.

New rules

Once you've prepared yourself physically and emotionally for your entry back into the dating world, it's wise to learn the basics of what has changed since you last dated. As I mentioned earlier, almost everything has changed, from how you find and meet someone, to attitudes, sexual etiquette, and even money matters.

Some of these changes may be difficult for a later dater to deal with because they grew up in other eras and with other social rules. But it's like any other venture. Don't get into it without researching what it takes to make it work for you.

Here are a few pointers that are expanded upon in later chapters.

Attitudes

The basic difference between dating when youthful and dating as a later dater is that, generally speaking, most later daters (of both sexes) are not necessarily looking for marriage. They may not be averse to cohabiting but many later daters have already been there, done that, and bear the scars.

Above all, they're looking for someone compatible that they can enjoy life with: someone they can spend time with and talk to. Someone who will share their particular lifestyle, the pleasures of their family and friends, their hopes and dreams.

Many are looking for a relationship that may or may not include sex. The latter may be for reasons of health, lack of ability, or lack of interest.

On the other hand, many later daters are looking for just that: an active sex life. It's wise for any person dating later in life to decide what it is they personally want from a new relationship and whether sex is going to be a part of that decision.

If you are only looking for companionship, then, in fairness to the other person, you should make it clear right from the start of the relationship. It can be very hurtful to a person who wants a full, sexually active relationship to find that the time spent meeting and nurturing a liaison, while not exactly wasted, doesn't help develop the relationship to the point they require.

That doesn't exactly mean you have to announce that you aren't interested in sex in the first ten minutes of the first date (unless you want to end the date there and then). But making the fact known in early conversation that your quest is for companionship ensures that this new person can then decide if this will meet his needs or not.

Making what you're looking for clear from the start is not being "pushy" or demanding, it's being straightforward and practical, as well as considerate.

When you were young and single, you may not have been fully aware of what you wanted out of life and from a partner and, anyway, you had a whole life ahead of you to sort it out. Dating in mid or late life means you should know by now (as should the men you meet) and not feel embarrassed about being honest about what and whom you are looking for.

Costs

Another area where the rules of dating have changed is that of dating costs. In past eras, it was always the man who paid, sometimes for everything.

We live in very different times, now, especially for the later dater.

Women are often financially independent by this time of their lives. They may be in a career, job, or own their own business in which they manage their own finances and have their own incomes. They may have received settlements in divorces or have inherited money from family. They might also not be in a good financial situation and are hoping for a wealthy "white knight" to arrive and save them. (Good luck with that because there are many women of all ages hoping for that fantasy to happen. And dating in mid and late life can be an expensive undertaking for both sexes.) But, whatever the situation, many women may possibly be worth as much financially or be earning the same or more than the single men they meet.

In dating, it's not a question of who has more money; it's a general contemporary agreement that costs are shared 50/50. And a very basic rule (and rules, like promises, are often broken) is that the person who issues the invitation for a date pays.

In the case of a man's offering to pay for the first date, whether dinner, movie drinks, coffee, or what have you, the woman should immediately offer to pay her half. This is especially correct if you're on a blind date or are meeting someone for the first time from, say, an online dating site.

If he refuses, and many older men are insistent on paying because they often feel humiliated and emasculated if they don't, the woman should offer to cover the costs "next time."

This has two effects. One is that you assert your independence and pride; the other is that you show that you are interested in this person (if you actually are) and wish to have another date with him. If you're not interested or perhaps got the impression he isn't either, still state this, however. It's a polite way of exiting and parting on good terms .

Insisting that a man pay for everything is not only old-fashioned but very selfish.

Equality between the sexes has also changed the face of dating. We may be more mature and dating late, but we're living in the 21st century where equality rules. No longer do women wait to be asked out on date or wait for a drink to be offered when the situation arises. Nor do they (or should they) be constantly checking their cell phone for "that" call or text. They can make the first call if they like; ask a man out on a date; offer a man a drink; tip the barperson, waitperson, or coat attendant; call the cab; and take charge in whatever situation that, in the old days, was always left to the man while the woman waited patiently on the side.

That doesn't mean you need to be aggressive or overly assertive in a way that offends or irritates. Taking charge in some areas of dating is the contemporary way, and most older men are quite comfortable with (and often admire) a woman who knows how to handle herself and her life with confidence, style, and panache. That is, unless they've been living alone on a remote island for the past three decades.

It doesn't mean women have taken over men's roles in life. It means they share everything, including responsibility.

Chapter Two

Ready, Willing, and Able

So now you're a ready, willing, and able later dater. Fully prepared, physically and emotionally, you're eager to embark on your explorative journey.

But how and where do you start? Where do you go to meet single older men, especially because it isn't so easy to connect with anyone, let alone a single male later dater these days? These are, perhaps obviously, the most frequent questions asked by single women who are available and looking for a relationship in mid and late life.

In years past, all it took was an eager, supportive, and active network of family, friends, and colleagues. If asked, they were constantly on the lookout for a single man (sometimes any single man…) they might think would suit you and your situation.

Even though the men they introduced you to were, in fact, often totally unsuitable — which led you to wonder how people you'd known most, if not all, your life, could get your needs and desires so terribly wrong — they were at least actively involved. It also meant you had to go on a number of those infamous "blind dates" — awkward, often excruciating evenings during which you frantically wondered how the heck you were going to escape quickly without offending the date and, later, the friends or family who set you up.

If there's one lesson I've learned in a busy, active dating life, it's that only a very tiny percent of blind dates work.

There are obviously a number of reasons for a blind date's failure. But a major reason is that both participants probably have hopeful, perhaps idealized ideas of the person they have never met because whoever arranged the date has waxed lyrical about both party's looks, personality, intelligence, and achievements. So, unless you're a Julianne Moore lookalike and he's a George Clooney clone, expectation levels (and perhaps fantasies) can be too high to be realistically met. Or it just may be intense dislike (or at least disappointment) on sight. (Yes, it happened to me once, and the feeling was apparently mutual — an unpleasant experience!)

But the truth is, rarely will someone else find you a date. Family members, friends, and colleagues are so overwhelmingly busy and stressed these days, they simply don't have the time to spend on a search for someone for you. You'll find that occasionally someone will say, "I know just the man for you," but, almost always, nothing ever comes of it, despite your prodding.

What's more, regularly reminding them that you are "still looking," can become irritating and they will avoid the subject, and perhaps you too, if you keep on about it.

Most people view someone's search for a date or partner as private business and no one else's and don't feel it's their place to interfere. And, after all, it might take up too much of their time and attention anyway.

Yet it still remains a positive move to network and let everyone know initially that you are now ready to date someone or ask them to keep an eye open for an available single, older man who might be suitable. But then leave the subject alone. To be honest, apart from perhaps a close friend or two, you're on your own.

A good initial tip is to accept every invitation you receive and seek out others, whether to a party, business function, art opening, charity event, or group get-together and whether or not you know anyone who'll be there. One of the skills you will have to learn, if you don't know it already, is not only how to attend functions on your own and mingle well with other guests, but, most important, how to enjoy yourself even though you're alone.

And I know it sounds a little offbeat, but you'd be surprised how many single men you can meet at a funeral. I know because I've met some very pleasant men a few times at such somber events.

Since most female later daters dislike going to bars, even with a group, and there are few, if any, public night clubs for people over 30 and certainly none for those over 50 that offer an interesting, vibrant yet relaxed atmosphere for meeting people, we need to explore other alternatives.

Singles organizations for the 50-plus are an area of business that has sprung up in recent years in response to the increasing number of older singles searching for each other or just interested in getting together. These organizations cover a wide spectrum of activities and hobbies — dances, dinners, travel, hiking, skiing, and more, sometimes offering regular events throughout the year. The number of such organizations available generally depends on the size of the area in which you live and whether or not you are close to a town or city.

A travel business no longer needs to be in an office, and many singles organizations have a vast Internet network in many cities. Other travel companies are also very aware of the vast number of mid- and late-life singles who want to see the world. You may wince at some of the companies' names because they include terms such as "elder" or "senior," but swallow your pride and ignore that fact because they offer trips specifically designed for those who are older than the youthful backpacker.

These companies make everything easy for you, taking into consideration factors such as your ability to walk long distances or not, or whether you are able to climb or hike rough terrain. They also offer extra comforts such as home pick-ups and take care of every detail, both financial and physical.

Most groups are a mix of men and women, and while it's true a number of them will be couples, I've known several women who have met splendid partners on such trips, especially cruises.

There's no question that when you're doing something you enjoy, you become interesting to other people involved, including single men. While the singles travel group may not change over time unless there's a constant flow of members, at least you all share a common interest and can get to know each other well.

Above all, with singles organizations in your area, you can generally be sure that everyone is single. A hazard of dating at later ages is the married person (both male and female) looking for an affair. These folks are more difficult to detect (but more on dealing with that later).

Other group activities that can be beneficial not only to meeting the opposite sex but also to your health and mind are educational courses or learning a new skill. Classes or seminars that can interest men, such as technology, finances, and investing, are a good bet for a later dater looking to meet single men, as are courses to either learn or brush up on another language. The latter can also be useful for travel, if you're so inclined.

Older men these days are also very interested in wine, gardening, cookery, art, and even yoga and self-improvement classes. Or try an activity that requires you to physically interact, such as dancing.

It perhaps goes without saying that interactive sports (golf, skiing, bowling, and more) are another area of strong male interest — particularly worthwhile if you are searching for someone who is reasonably fit and active. But be sure to be reasonably fit yourself if you are insisting on meeting such a man because they almost always require a partner who can keep up with them and even challenge them!

Joining a fitness club for mature adults (there are increasing numbers of such businesses opening now that they've realized demand is there and the size of the market) will ensure that the age group is suitable and help you meet someone who likes to stay in shape and is interested in health matters.

If joining such groups is beyond your budget, enquire about your local mall-walking groups, which are especially useful if your winter is a long, cold one, or hiking groups.

Volunteering for charity is a wonderful way to feel good about yourself and perhaps meet another later dater. While most volunteers tend to be female, I often point out to those single women who are dubious about this avenue that the women involved might know of a single older man (such as a brother, friend, or neighbour) who is also searching for a relationship.

Getting involved in your community has the same effect, with perhaps a more balanced number of men and women involved. This can be with your local ratepayers association, business organization, political group, for example.

And don't discount becoming a member of the fundraising committees of cultural institutions, such as your local art gallery, museum, or opera. You'll meet a mix of people who are deeply interested in culture. And because these organizations usually have a number of functions and fundraising events throughout the year, you'll be able to expand your social circle.

A great deal of your search will depend on the time available to you. You may be working in a full- or part-time job or running a business. Maybe may still have children at home, are helping out with your grandchildren, or are the chief caregiver for your ill or elderly parents. Your commitments can leave you with little spare time (and energy) to look around for a partner.

In the past, advertising for a partner in a newspaper's personal section was an acceptable route for those later daters willing to take the risk and spend the time to sort through the responses. But this method has in recent years lost its allure, generally speaking, probably because it was not only expensive but because the small advertisements didn't include photos and provided very little information, making responding to the ad a much bigger leap of faith than most single people wanted to take.

But there is always an exception. In her best-selling book, *The Roundheeled Woman: My Late-Life Adventures in Sex and Romance,* Jane Juska wrote about her experiences as a 66-year-old who placed a personal ad in the *New York Times Review of Books*. Her daring ad stated, "before I turn 67 — next March — I would like to have a lot of sex with a man I like. If you want to talk first, Trollope works for me."

She was inundated with responses, and the book chronicles her fascinating (and very active!) foray into the world of later dating and, especially, mid- and late-life sex.

We still see plenty of personal ads in newspapers and magazines, but many of them are considered suspect or dubious these days. In the UK, however, it's both an acceptable and preferred method of looking for a relationship, especially if you're over 50. Full pages are devoted to ads of mostly older folk looking for each other.

Another method that is experiencing increased business, especially from female later daters, is the professional matchmaking service — or as some prefer to be called these days, "executive personal search" agencies. The services offered vary from agency to agency, but most of them charge an amount of money for a certain number of "introductions." Others charge for a package or for a period of time such as six months or a year. Matchmaking services can be a nationwide franchise, a boutique service, or a one-person business. Some agencies or matchmakers just want to make money, while others really care about matching up single people. The latter usually has an owner who is proud of his/her reputation in the matchmaking business and in some cases, may even have made it into a celebrity cause. This is particularly prevalent in the United States in places such as New York, Chicago, Los Angeles, and Hollywood.

Some agencies purport to only connect with millionaires and billionaires. One such celebrity matchmaker "star" charges over $150,000 US for their services. (No word on how many millionaires or billionaires are actually on her books.)

Costs vary of course, but generally speaking, personal search firms will price their services between $2,000 and $25,000. While some agencies have you sit with a book of photos of people so that you can point out any you might be attracted to (a haphazard method that you could do cheaper online), a good matchmaker or agency will meet with you in person to find out all they can about your interests, goals, likes, dislikes, dreams, career or life aspirations, family situation, the type of person you're looking for in a relationship and, of course, to see what you really look like and what kind of personality you have. At the end, they'll have a very comprehensive idea of who you're searching for and what you expect.

Again, if you go into this expecting the matchmaker to instantly find a George Clooney who will immediately fall for you, you're wasting your time and money. Thorough advanced searches take time, and the matchmaker may have to gently guide you towards a more suitable match by introducing you to men who didn't quite fit your original stringent requirements. One successful matchmaker owner I know actually found her own husband through her business and she says he didn't fit her criteria of a partner for her in any category whatsoever. Yet she fell in love with this "lovely man" and they are now very happily married.

She says that the major problem she faces with female later daters is their unrealistic expectations: "If they had more of an open mind and willingness to consider prospects who don't necessarily meet their overly high, and often unrealistic, expectation level, they just might meet that special partner."

However, for increasing numbers of later daters, the answer to many of the difficulties finding and learning something about a potential date before actually meeting face to face is the Internet. In other words, online dating.

Chapter Three

Online Dating

Love it or loathe it, online dating has become the most popular and most accessible method of connecting in the brave new world of Boomer and beyond singles. And, for many, it's the only means of connecting with each other.

In the early days online dating was sneered at or ignored. But that was the past; it no longer has the stigma of "last hope" and is a worldwide fully acceptable phenomenon. In the US alone, over 40 million people (of all ages) are dating online (onlineschools.org).

While there's no question online dating can be easy, safe, and rewarding, it can also be frustrating, expensive, and a minefield of misrepresentation. Yet no other method can so successfully connect a later dater with so many other singles in their preferred age range, both internationally and locally, than online dating.

Although it may look like dating sites are mostly populated by 25- to 35-year-olds, the prominent sites report that the biggest and fastest growing demographic of members is those over 50. Because of these growing numbers, many sites now have a specialty section for such age groups, and some sites cater solely to this demographic.

Most online daters will admit that the process can be very time consuming, with the constant checking of profiles and photos, and can also be very addictive. This can result in getting ODD (online dating dilemma), the constant and insidious wondering whether there is someone better a click away even though you've just connected with someone who might be a very suitable prospect.

This addictive dilemma is, of course, not exclusive to women. Members of both sexes risk becoming fixated on the technological dating method. There may also be as many female "serial online daters" (those who go online just to get a weekly/monthly date with no intention of forming a relationship) as male, but as a general rule, most later dater women who join online dating sites are serious and are earnestly looking for a relationship.

Without doubt, online dating offers a large number of benefits to the later dater that, in today's hectic and often perfunctory face-to-face world, far outweigh trying to meet someone randomly in everyday life. The biggest benefit for Boomers and beyond is that it can be carried out easily from the comfort of your own home.

Online dating means:

- you can wear any old outfit, be without makeup, have unshaved legs, and messy hair while waxing lyrical about your good looks. Unless, of course, you opt to video-chat via Skype.

- you're tapping into a vast pool of single men you would never normally meet who are also looking for that special someone (at least that's the premise on which online dating is based). What's more, you can search a preferred age range and find a large selection to choose from and approach.

- you can narrow your search and learn whether someone is suitable for you by discovering a person's values, goals, hobbies, background, lifestyle, and financial and family status well before you actually decide to meet them in person.

- is dating with dignity because you're at a venue of your own choice (at home or anywhere you wish logging in with your tech device) and are searching entirely at your convenience.

- no more indignities of going to bars, clubs or events that don't cater to your age group and which always seem to be packed with 20- to 30-somethings, half of whom appear to be fashion models.

- you're in complete control of choosing and contacting someone and accepting or rejecting those who contact you.

- you're relatively anonymous because you don't have to disclose your address or phone number or even your name to anyone until you choose to (or at least until you've met them in person and decide that it's the next step).

- you can state specifically in your profile the kind of person you're looking for and the kind of person you are yourself. You can then select someone from their profile and their photograph (which are both hopefully up-to-date). This information can be expanded after the initial contact and through email, telephone, or Skype, all before actually meeting them physically and without any commitment.

- allows you to waste less time and obtain more information you did with the old method of starting from scratch with the first hello and going through, as one man said with a sigh, "the endless repeating of your own history."

Online dating basically offers a huge catalogue of hopefully receptive single men at your fingertips.

Which is why I call it the Shopping Channel.

Let's be honest. Aren't we shopping for a mate when we scour through hundreds of photos and profiles looking for a potential companion? It may sound cynical but it's actually being realistic and practical. And realistic and practical is exactly what you have to be so that you not only get the best out of online dating but also survive it emotionally and ultimately achieve success.

Despite all the advantages of online dating, there are still a few pitfalls. While online dating can be conducted from the comfort of your own home, it will still take considerable time and some money to be thorough — and successful — in your search.

Although online dating appears to be cloaked by anonymity, it's really very similar, in most facets, to face-to-face dating. Online dating is more focused and detailed than conventional dating and is much trickier to navigate.

Also, the cloak of anonymity can lead to misrepresentation. Photos may be old, out of date, or retouched; ages may be lessened by a few (or many) years; height, weight, profession, and income may be more aspirational than actual truth.

According to onlineschools.org, who have researched online dating, men lie about their age, while women lie about their weight. Such stretching of the truth will, obviously, become apparent when you meet someone, or very soon thereafter. Yet, despite this very obvious point, misrepresentations persist.

You may wonder why. Such people may possibly have the illusion that you will fall madly in love with their vibrant personality as soon as you meet them, despite their blatant fudging of the facts. They're wrong and are setting themselves up for continued rejection or anger from those who have been misled.

Honesty is the best, and only, policy for online dating.

Starting Out

Although you may want to look through a number of general dating sites because they may have a large number of later dater members or have a sub-site for older people, you might find it more effective to concentrate on sites that specifically cater to later daters.

Search the web using key words such as "50 plus online dating" or "senior singles online dating" (even if you bristle at the thought of using the word "senior," it does direct you to the pertinent sites). Then research each website to see which format appeals to you and before you pay any membership money. Most sites allow limited browsing for free.

An astonishing number of "specialty" dating sites cater to people of specific ethnic, culture, religion, hobby, or personal interests (from everyday to wildly way out there) who are looking for someone with particular traits or interests to date or befriend.

A few sites have an overly large quota of single older women as members. You may find it worthwhile to improve your odds of finding someone by choosing a site that appears to have a reasonable number of men in the specific age group you're interested in. Statistics show that there are more men than women dating online, so the odds are in your favor.

Although some sites encourage women to join for free, those may not be the sites you want. For instance, I once checked out a site where women could join for free that I thought sounded perfect by its title for meeting older, established men only to find it was for those wanting to be "sugar daddies" for younger women!

Another important point is to check the membership cost and cancellation policy of a site before plunging in, just as you would if you were joining a fitness club. If you feel you want to research further and read some reviews, a number of websites specialize in reviewing online dating sites. For instance, datingsitesreviews.com gives comprehensive reviews for Canadian, UK, and Australian sites, while datingsitesreviews4u.com deals with the US and datingsitesweb.co.uk covers the UK. The website edatereview.com asks for personal reviews of dating sites by members or former members, which makes for informative reading.

Despite the fact that online dating has now been established and accepted socially for more than a decade, older men and women often have a strong opinion, either negative or positive, of the process. It seems that they either like it and embrace it fully, fear and avoid it, or intensely dislike what they consider to be an electronic meat market full of dishonest people.

But with the right approach, a good attitude, and some basic knowledge of how to make it work, you can succeed at online dating.

Many people know, or at least have heard of, a couple who met through an online dating site and many who have subsequently married. It's getting more common, especially for later daters who, in the past, were shut out of such freedom of choice and ability to connect. So, no more excuses. All they do is hold you back from living life to the fullest.

Lynne, 54, an experienced online dater, stays she doesn't know a person who is single who isn't dating online. A tall, glamorous, fit blonde and a successful marketing professional, she says she's online because she doesn't meet anyone in her busy business world who appears to be both single and available.

"How do you know if anyone is single?" she asks. "They don't know I'm single either — we're there for business purposes. With online dating I can literally dial up the exact type of man I'm looking for."

The Photo

For the majority of online daters, a photo is essential. "No photo, no response," Lynne states.

So, once you've found the site that you feel suits your needs and attitudes, decide on a photograph that best represents you. You can use one you already have or you can get a capable friend or a professional to take one for you.

Of course, pick a photo that is flattering and makes you look as attractive as possible. Take some time over choosing it. Using a quick snapshot taken at the mall by a pal or a fuzzy vacation picture in which you're the small figure in front of a large scenic view is being lazy and won't get you the replies you deserve.

Don't use a group photo because it takes the focus and attention away from you. And don't use a photo where you've obviously cut away or faded out a past boyfriend or ex-husband. It indicates you that haven't fully moved on.

Your photo should be full length and show you clearly with a pleasant smile. Seasoned online daters mistrust headshots, often with good reason. An attractive face may be topping a body that shows that the person is not being truthful in their profile about the shape they're in. One handsome headshot I contacted and met while researching this book didn't indicate that he was very overweight and could hardly walk up steps. I had asked for "healthy, fit, and active." It can be extremely disappointing for someone looking for a healthy and active partner to discover that they'd been misled.

If, however, you're not bothered by shape, weight, size, or fitness ability, don't discount headshots. But to get more response to your own photo, make sure it is full-length.

And, very important, choose a photo for the site that shows how you look now, not how you looked in your 30s.

User Name

This will be your dating site moniker or membership ID. It should be anonymous, but still say something about you. It could refer to your hobby, such as "NatureLover," or perhaps about your personality, such as

Fun&Spirited. Think carefully about the words that describe you perfectly.

Subject line

The subject line is usually a very short headline on your profile that

says a little more about you. Keep your subject line positive, even fun. Ask

yourself who you are. Do your friends think you're outgoing? cheerful?

charming? sporty? Do you like to laugh and love life? How about

affectionate or adventurous?

Don't be overtly sexual, too romantic, or critical of men in your

choice of words. What you want is to catch the eye of someone who might

share the qualities you have or have those that are compatible.

Profile

A well-put-together profile is as important as a good photo. Writing a

profile unsettles women who aren't used to promoting themselves in any

way except in person (if then). But a number of sites offer help in creating a

"good" profile, one that will bring you the most responses from the men you

might be interested in.

Some sites only require profiles that you can do in minutes, while others want you to fill out a lengthy and time-consuming questionnaire. Choose a site that makes you feel comfortable with the amount of information you need to give about yourself.

Profiles should be upbeat, honest, optimistic, and to the point. Later dater men want to meet a woman who appears interesting, active, healthy, fun to be with, and enthusiastic about life and whatever she does, for work or leisure. The best profiles have an interesting mixture of playful and serious.

But the truth is, people who are using online dating sites usually browse quickly because they're busy. If you don't catch their eye with a photo or a good subject line and a cheerful, well-written profile, you'll be left behind as they move onto another photo and profile.

Tips

- While your passion may be cats, it's far better to simply state you love animals. Whether we cat ladies like it or not, "loves cats" is apparently a major red flag to a male online dater, who perhaps imagines a house full of rescued strays wandering everywhere. He may crazy about dogs, anyway.

- Don't be too sexy, romantic, or anti-male in any way, about exes or anyone else. If it's too sexy and suggestive, yes, you'll have plenty of replies, but not the kind you want. If it's too romantic, you'll comes across as naïve and too needy. Male bashing totally defeats your purpose. Even the slightest suggestion of having been "burned" by men in the past will close the response door. Men like women who like men. It's that simple.

- Don't sound desperate, anxious, or despairing because you'll send up a red flag immediately. Men are not online to rescue someone.

- Although you may be able to shave a few years off your age and a few pounds off your weight, it's still best to be truthful or at least close. You won't be able to hide it once you've met, and some later daters you meet might even be angry and upset that you've wasted their time by lying. They may even wonder what else you haven't been honest about.

It's a fallacy that all men are looking for a size six. It's okay to be, as a beautiful, plus-size friend of mine always states, big, bold, and beautiful. It's a matter of presenting (or marketing) yourself by featuring your best assets.

It's also not true that all older men are looking for a much younger woman. In my experience, the majority of later dater men are looking for someone close to their own age. Someone they can relate to and who's had similar experiences in life, has similar goals for their later years, and understands the highs and lows of the adventure of getting older — in other words, someone who is a good match physically and emotionally.

Above all, they want someone they can love and who will reciprocate their affection, someone who will be supportive, be their friend and lover, and who will share and enjoy this special time of their life with them — which, after all, is what later dater women are looking for as well.

Okay, so it's true that some older men are also looking for a woman to look after them physically and, others, financially. If this isn't what you want, even if you're very nurturing or wealthy, be aware and do your research before you meet them. Or, if that isn't possible or doesn't work, ask the pertinent questions that will give you an indication as to their personal and financial situation. After all, you'd do the same if you were applying for a job or meeting an employer or employee. Learn to adopt the same businesslike attitude. As Lynne says, "Online dating (in the later dater field) is very competitive. You have to be on the top of your game if you want to meet someone these days."

The Search

All online dating sites have systems that will automatically match you up according to your member criteria, where you live, and how close or far you are willing to search. You can regulate how often you receive these "matches."

You obviously have by now a good idea of the type of man you're searching for, but that doesn't mean that you should just skim through the photos and not read the profiles.

Profiles will tell you a lot about the man: his interests, views, goals, ethnicity (if important), family and job situation; whether he's retired, a widower, or lifelong bachelor; income and education; his astrological sign; and more — all important details to varying degrees.

Bear in mind that the income details may or may not be true. Most men want to be known as successful, so you'll find out more when you know where he lives, what he does, and so on. Also, you are probably interested in an age group in which most men are retired or retiring, so income may not be indicative of current lifestyle.

Lynne says she always Googles the man's name once she knows it, but her dates are usually top executives in a high income bracket so it's easier to find out information about them than about the average man.

But it's still wise to learn as much as possible about an online prospect before giving out vital information about yourself, such as an address or phone number. Spotting aspects of a man's character from a profile isn't too difficult. Bad spelling and grammar, for instance, is not indicative of a well-educated, intelligent, experienced man, if that is the type you're looking for. Any sexual innuendo is a no-no as are comments that are derogatory to women. Men who make such comments should be avoided.

Also, be a little wary if the profile states that the man is "separated." Although it can indeed be an honest statement, far too often it means that someone is looking for an affair and that they are still attached, or even living with their wife. It's up to you whether you want to explore such a situation further or avoid it altogether (see Chapter 4).

Again, it's difficult to tell this from a profile he wrote, of course, and may mean that when you meet someone for the first time, you'll have to ask some subtle questions in order to check this out for sure.

If the man offers a number of excuses as to why he can't tell you about his past, he might have something to hide. If he is furtive about telling you where he lives, gives you only his cell number and not his home phone number, and states that he is only available during the week and never on weekends, it's possible that he's married or living with someone.

Keep your financial information to yourself until you know the date better, and don't give out your address, just the general area where you live, until you're sure of the person. Later daters have usually built up their assets and, although it seems to happen often, this is not the time of life to lose any of them to someone unscrupulous. Be very cautious and aware, and if your instincts tell you something's not quite right, trust them.

If you feel you really want the goods on someone you've met and liked but your antennae are tingling, you might want to take things even further and have the man investigated. There are companies that specialize in cyber-cases such as DateSmart.com, whose slogan is, "If you date, investigate" and whose website offers a dozen helpful "red flags" that may alert you to someone who is being dishonest or hiding the truth from you.

Don't rush into anything with your new relationship. Spend time chatting via the site, email, or phone before setting up a meeting. Texting can give too little information. You can tell a lot from a voice or what they write and, although it doesn't tell you if there is any chemistry between the two of you and doesn't trump meeting face to face, it's an essential start.

When the time comes to meet in person, be sure to choose a public place such as a local café or a popular bar or restaurant.

Lynne says she prefers to go for a drink or dinner rather than for coffee, but it's a question of preference and how comfortable you feel meeting a relative stranger. Dinner is a big step with someone you don't know. You may dislike each other and it can be agonizing to have to spend an evening together in such circumstances. I've heard quite a number of horror stories of women escaping from a bad dinner date in wild and weird ways.

My own preference is to get through a not-so-good experience and make a good excuse to leave as soon as you reasonably can. But I've always believed in being polite and courteous and thanking the date, no matter what. You can always decline any further invitations later.

Make sure you let a close friend or family member know where you're going and ask them to check in at a set time. It may seem overly cautious, but you're meeting someone alone for the first time, someone with whom you may have connected with only by voice or email.

This is where systems such as Skype work well. You get to see the person live and can gain more information from actually viewing them and conversing with them in real time. It enables you to decide for sure whether this is a person you want to get to know better or not.

And take your time, even after you've met him and think he's perfect. One of the major complaints from men who are dating online is about women who want to get serious too fast.

So who are the men you might meet when dating online, or via any other method?

While there is, of course, every type of man you can imagine, the next chapter presents some recognizable outlines of the different kinds of later dater men you might expect to meet as you propel yourself into the dating arena.

Chapter Four

The Dating Lottery

Looking for someone new when you're 50-plus can be exciting, interesting, and often fascinating as you meet a variety of different single men who are (mostly) in the same boat as you. This basically means, of course, that the odds are pretty good that you'll meet someone who'll appeal to you and who will return your interest.

That's the theory, of course.

Yes, it can feel like looking for a needle in a haystack and can be discouraging, but at least the odds are far better than the lottery. With dating, you have the means and ability to narrow down the odds to be in your favour.

One way to do this is universally understood. Most women search for a man they feel is their "type." And, whatever your type, in order to succeed, you have to believe he's out there somewhere, even if finding him is the gambling aspect of dating, which can be, admittedly, frustrating as you sift through the prospects. But it can ultimately be very rewarding.

And although every person is obviously a unique individual, there are some general "types" you may meet or encounter as you plunge enthusiastically into the dating arena.

Divorced or Separated (legally or otherwise)

This is by far the largest category of single men you will meet as a later dater, especially "divorced."

With more and more divorces occurring late in life, particularly in long-term marriages, it's pretty much inevitable that the man you'll meet will have been married, perhaps not just once but maybe twice or even several times. With people living much longer and having far more options in life, this is no longer so unusual, neither for men nor women.

Divorced men generally fall into one of two categories: those who have had, or are having, an amicable divorce (or divorces); and those who are or were in a bitter and acrimonious situation.

Naturally, the man who has had or is in the middle of an amicable divorce proceeding will, generally speaking, be less stressed, more pleasant, and more easygoing dating material, but, as you may already know from your own situation, if you're a divorcee, an amicable situation can turn into a bitter fight at any moment. And if it does, the cause is usually connected to money, possessions, children, or even pets, which just about covers everything.

But the man who has had an amicable divorce doesn't usually have a hurt, bitter, angry, or jealous ex lurking in the background. In my experience, it can also mean there aren't any young children involved either. When there are, and it is still amicable, then the best scenario is that these are two extremely balanced, intelligent, reasonable parents concerned for their children's welfare

Also the amicably divorced man will usually have a reasonable opinion of women and treat his ex-wife and other women with respect — very important traits in the male species, at no matter what age — and extremely important to later daters.

Of course, a great deal of amicability will depend on whether the divorce was by mutual agreement or whether one made the split and chose to leave the other. It will then depend on whether they left for someone else, which doesn't usually produce an amiable situation unless both partners have someone else in their lives. There may be, of course, underlying or outward rivalry. The complexities of other people's convoluted past relationships can be a tricky-to-navigate obstacle course.

If a date has gone through a bitter divorce, be prepared to be the nurturing sounding board for his frustrations. These can be particularly acute if the divorce is relatively recent and he is still mentally (and probably financially) reeling from the experience.

Tip: Never agree with him when he criticizes his ex, probably with an often-embellished story of her wanton and willful ways. In fact, do not give any opinion beyond "I'm sorry to hear that" or similar soothing phrases. If the date or dates with him become an endless raging about his ex, then don't go on another one and just say, "Perhaps you're not quite ready to date just yet?"

Of course, it may go without saying, but I am going to say it anyway, when you are dating someone new, you also do not rage and rant about your ex or even continuously talk about him. Your new date will obviously want to know something about your previous partner, but keep it very basic, informative, and light, and do not tear him to pieces verbally because you think it will be encouraging. It won't be and, in fact, may guarantee that you don't get a second date.

An important question to ask a new date when he announces he is divorced is "When did it happen"? The answer will give you some idea of where he is emotionally at the moment. Obviously the more time that has passed since the divorce, the more time he has had to adjust to his new way of life and, especially, the reality of being single again. He may relish it, merely endure it, or dislike it intensely. All have a bearing on how eager he is to date and find someone new and, if that's is what you're looking for, whether or not he wants another committed relationship.

If he is just out of a divorce, he may be emotionally fragile. It's up to you to decide whether he is ready to start another relationship so soon. Many aren't ready until they've had some time to adjust and deal with their emotions and new lifestyle. It will, of course, depend on how long the divorce proceedings have been going on because some can drag on for years, in which case he'll have had plenty of opportunity to come to terms with everything and know what he wants.

In some cases, he may also still be in love with his ex-wife, or not ready to move on, which you can figure out quite quickly when you converse about your pasts and your experiences. This can be an uphill battle to overcome, and you may not want to spend effort on what possibly could be, in the end, a losing proposition for you if you don't measure up to the "jewel" of an ex.

Separated

Dating a separated man can be more hazardous than dating one who is divorced, because he might be on a "trial" separation, which some men take to be a licence to go out and be wildly single to see what he missed while in a committed relationship or marriage. He may decide to return to that relationship, depending on which partner wanted the trial separation and what his experiences were as a temporarily single man.

It's also possible that a separated man is not really separated at all but is playing the field while having a safe haven of a wife or partner at home to run to if he finds being "single" doesn't work out too well for him.

Men in that situation may be a little freer than the married man who is out cheating but will still be wary at being caught at their game.

Some men who are separated are genuine and may be working on a divorce or legal separation agreement. It is wise, if at times a little difficult with someone you may have just met and dated, to find out a few details of his situation and judge for yourself.

Most men (and women) are only too happy to talk about their current situation at the beginning of a new relationship, so if he shows considerable reluctance to do so, maybe he has something to hide.

As with recently divorced men, recently separated men can be emotionally fragile or perhaps too eager to jump into a physical relationship. They sometimes want to prove they "still have it" or want to flaunt their success with women at their separated partner. The problem here may be that you could be just one of a number of women on whom he is testing out his newfound freedom.

Widower

This is an obvious category in the later dater world and one that is most sought after by many female later daters for a number of valid reasons, especially if she herself has been widowed. If, for instance, the man was in a long-term marriage with a woman he loved dearly, he might be one of the best men to date and form a new relationship with. He could be a treasure because, generally speaking, he understands commitment; giving and receiving love over a long period; domesticity; and the demands, ebb and flow, and ups and downs of a real relationship.

If the marriage wasn't a happy one, however, he may be overeager to jump into a new one.

He may also be used to having someone look after him, and if he has health problems, he might be looking for someone to take care of him in his later years. In my experience, very few female later daters want to be someone's nurse in exchange for companionship. (Of course, if he's a 90-year-old ailing billionaire . . .)

On the other hand, he may not have loved his departed wife, but be certain she will still be a "wonderful" ex now that's she's gone.

A drawback for a later dater dating a widower who was very attached to his departed wife might be his still strong devotion to her. His home, for instance, might be full of photos of them together, which he intends to keep in place.

Some widowers don't realize how discouraging it is for someone to visit their new date's home and find it looks like a shrine to another woman, especially in the bedroom. I experienced this once and was very uncomfortable with it. I felt she was watching. Be particularly wary if the closet is still filled with her clothes long after her passing.

A plus for lady later daters is that most older widowers often prefer a woman similar in age either to himself or his late wife. But if he felt trapped in his marriage, he could now feel he's been released. He may therefore hanker after much younger women because he's fighting to get back those lost years. The latter is a very common scenario and, depending on age, health, and financial situation, can be hazardous and short-lived for him when the young woman inevitably moves on.

Peter Pans

A later dater undoubtedly will meet a Peter Pan at some point along the dating road. While obviously not exclusive to the male species, Peter Pans refuse to acknowledge their age or other age-related drawbacks and will, by any means, attempt to prolong any youth they feel they still have. This can manifest itself in their noticeably dyeing their hair; wearing too youthful clothing, getting cosmetically nipped and tucked, and behaving as though they were half their age.

While in some men, this can be endearing and even amusing, most lady later daters don't find it attractive or suitable, mainly because Peter Pans are in the category of looking for and, in some cases, dating much younger women, believing it will renew their youth and keep old age at bay. It may work for a short time but in the long term, it doesn't last and they can end up very lonely men in their latter days.

The Never Married

It's surprising how many men are still unmarried at a late stage of their life. While there can be many valid reasons why a man has reached his later days without marrying, and they will often insist they "haven't met the right one along the way," it usually is a red flag for later daters looking for a solid relationship.

Perhaps these men are petrified of commitment or are unable to give real love and affection to another person. They may be latent gays who are unwilling to face reality and who struggle with their true desires. They may still be living at home with their elderly parent or parents, emotionally unable to leave them and afraid to forge a life for themselves. They may have lived with their mother to whom they have a deep attachment but who has passed on (yet they still live the same life as though she were still at home). They may have mental health issues that have held them back from getting close to a woman, or anyone else.

As I said earlier, there are undoubtedly some valid reasons for men to be unmarried late in life, but as a general rule, such men are not suitable for any later dater who wants a close and lasting relationship, and, in particular, marriage. If he hasn't been there by now, he never will be.

Don Juans

Don Juans have much in common with Peter Pans, but the age factor of who they chase is more flexible. Usually called womanizers, these men believe they're the answer to every women's romantic and sexual dreams. While they may be skilled flirts, which can be fun and flattering for a short while, it soon becomes obvious that they will flirt with, and date, most women they meet who are single and available — as well as those who are not.

Don Juans can be narcissistic playboy wannabes looking for sex and wanting to bolster their image and reputation. They're also likely to be dating a number of women at one time, women who may not suspect their date is a serial Don Juan.

It can be a shock when a woman find out the unsettling fact her new man has multiple partners plus, of course, the realization that the situation can become a very real sexual hazard (more on this in Chapter 6).

Dating a Don Juan can be fun and exciting for a time, but you need to beware of falling for one and be aware that you may not be the only one he's seeing, despite his protestation that he "adores" you and his apparent sincerity that he "is a gentleman and would do no such thing."

Serial daters

Serial daters go from one date to another mainly because they can do so very easily, especially online. These are men who actively use the fact that they can operate without scrutiny and without being found out while on one dating site — or several. Serial daters contact someone for a date, say on a Saturday, then after it is over, go back online and get another for the next weekend. And so on. The women they date, perhaps only once or twice, are upset because they wonder what went wrong and often blame themselves. Admittedly, the serial dater, particularly online, isn't so prevalent in older men.

Rich Men/Poor Men

It might seem to some to be a clear choice, but in love and later dating, matters can get muddied when it comes to money.

Whether the financial situation of the date, good or bad, matters greatly to a later dater depends on a number of factors, mostly her own finances. A wealthy or well-established later dater is usually searching for someone in a similar financial situation, because she feels someone who is on an equal financial footing will fit in her current lifestyle and fit in with her friends and family.

Many female later daters are very cautious and want to know about the finances of someone they meet because they certainly don't want to meet anyone unscrupulous who might merely be after her money.

Yet I have met later daters who have fallen in love with men who obviously didn't have as much money as they did and are quite comfortable with the situation. It often depends on the age of the partner (see Chapter 5) and also on how the later dater views her future, in particular, how much she values love and a relationship over material matters.

A word of warning: refusing to date anyone who isn't rich, established, and successful will not only narrow the field of prospects considerably, it may mean that you miss out on a wonderful, creative, loving man to whom wealth is not the most important factor in life.

Gays

This may seems an odd category for a heterosexual later dater and, in fact, doesn't really come under the heading of "dating" but more "close friendship."

But there's no question that, nowadays, many later daters have a wonderful gay friend who escorts them to parties and events, takes them out to dinner, and listens to their secrets as well as share his own. It does, of course, involve no sex or marriage (although such a union isn't totally unknown, either by mistake or arrangement), but no one will be more interested in your dating experiences and be happy to give advice (sometimes wildly wrong) about the relationships you encounter than your gay friend.

He will, most certainly, always want to give you a critique of what you're wearing and tell you whether it's suitable for your dating forays. Be wary if he insists you dress like Cher, however.

And of course, all this will be different if your date is another woman, whether for the first time or as a lifelong personal choice.

Chapter Five

Cougar or Conformist?

The majority of later daters are interested in a relationship with a man of similar or older age, but it's becoming more common for older women to date (and occasionally marry) younger men. This is not just because there is far more acceptance of an age gap or alternative relationship these days but because women's concept of aging and how they will approach it — and enjoy it — has changed dramatically.

Women have come to realize that, far from the indoctrination over the centuries, they aren't "finished" after menopause, particularly with regard to their sexuality and desirability and even their value to society. That belief was a result of patriarchal control and was historically tied to the fact that having numerous children was essential in days when many babies died young, often at birth. Men previously remarried to younger women who would give them children.

Also, in those days, both men and women died far younger, so therefore old age began far earlier. A woman of 50-plus today would have, in the past, been approaching the end of her life and would have been considered elderly.

Cheers for the twenty-first century!

People are living much longer and healthier lives and many women find that, although they may have been through menopause, it hasn't totally diminished their sexuality and certainly not their self-confidence. And if it has lowered their libido, they're taking either medical advice or herbal steps to remedy the situation.

It's also a fact that today's older women see their future in a positive light. They're often fit, strong, well-educated, independent, and full of optimism. They may be widowed or divorced, but they realize there is still a lengthy stretch of active life and good living to do and they intend to make the most of it.

Many also find that, far from what they've been led to believe over the centuries, their sexual energy and desire hasn't necessarily waned. It still exists, if more calm, manageable, and discerning, and they not only look and feel youthful but also sexy and desirable.

This new generation of interesting older women hasn't gone unnoticed by younger men.

When I wrote my book *Cougar* in 2001, older women dating younger men still had vestiges of taboo about it, with societal condemnation still very much in existence. There was strong feeling, oddly often from other women, that it "wasn't normal." Some even stated it was "disgusting," despite the fact that it was quite normal — even applauded — for men.

The result of such a lingering societal taboo was that vital, lively, confident, and sophisticated older women who attracted and dated younger men generally kept it secret from everyone except their closest friends.

The younger men who wanted to have a relationship with these exciting and challenging women also kept it quiet, hiding the relationship from their families and even their friends, who were often unable to understand the attraction.

The celebrity-driven public openness for women having younger beaus wasn't in full swing at that time and my book, by necessity, was based on the older woman who chose to pursue and instigate such a relationship. How times change!

There has been a complete turnaround in the trend in recent years, although I don't like calling it a trend because, in reality, the younger man/older woman relationship has been in existence since time began, albeit in secret. Younger men, fired with enthusiasm and the allure of a hitherto forbidden world, became the predators. Even more important to the youthful world was that it had now become "cool" to date a sexy single older woman. Hollywood stars and celebrities were dating or marrying younger men, and the media was beginning to see the age-gap relationship as newsworthy and entertaining. And interesting and sophisticated single older women found themselves suddenly being approached openly by younger men eager to date them, whether or not they themselves were interested.

Calling themselves "cougar hunters," these young men created websites and groups in celebration of dating older women, which in turn, encouraged more of them to pursue what, up until now, had just been their secret sexual fantasy.

For older women, the reversal in the trend from pursuer to pursued helped remove a barrier that had held many of them back from experiencing the excitement and energy of a younger partner. Many did not want to be seen as a "predator" or a "cougar" and therefore were viewed as visibly and openly challenging the ancient societal rule of men being in control of relationships by saying women could also take charge.

Yet they also realized that preferring to date younger meant they could have, perhaps for the first time in their lives, control of their sexual lives and were free to choose whoever they want in a relationship with them. Not the other way around.

A number of websites specifically target women who want to be proactive with their choice and don't want to wait to be approached by a younger man. Google "cougar dating" or "older women/younger men dating" and see if any of the sites are suitable for your needs. Then go and have fun!

But why choose younger when someone of your own age or older might better understand the experiences, pleasures, changes, and problems of being older? It is, after all, impossible for someone younger to do that because they haven't arrived there yet. But that's exactly the point, and one that older men have always understood. Having a younger person in their life and in their bed makes them feel youthful and alive again and often reignites their sexuality and vigor.

Dating younger is also a doorway to a completely new world, albeit one that perhaps can only be viewed from a distance by the older person. But being with a younger partner can certainly shorten that distance. Women who do date younger men find that it can be thrilling to be able to step back in time to a younger age, if only virtually, or embrace and learn from a current world that can, at times, seem to be racing by confusingly and at breakneck speed.

But, of course, there's far more to dating younger men than just jumping into and becoming part of their world. Many older women can do that through their grown children. And, for many later daters, dating younger doesn't suit them or their needs and desires and may be an area of dating they don't understand, or even want to understand.

But for those who do take up the challenge, dating younger can be a revelation and often life-changing.

Of the women who prefer to date younger or are attracted to that scenario, there's no question the majority find it exciting, stimulating, interesting, ego-boosting, and plain fun and sexy. Some assert it's the best and most satisfying relationship they've ever had.

Most women of 50, 60, and 70 may not choose a very young man to date, although, obviously, if you're 70 years old, a 60-year-old is a younger man! But it's entirely possible these days to date someone up to 20 years younger if you have the energy and stamina that matches theirs. Older men do it all the time.

Of course, it may be the other way around, with the older woman being the one who has the energy and stamina to spare. In fact, dating someone younger can often be strongly connected to finding someone who matches your own energy level and life outlook and requirements.

However, whether much younger or a ten-year-or-less difference, dating young men probably means a surge of sexual activity, depending on your age and their age.

While it may be unfamiliar territory at this stage of life, experiencing again the hot lust of sexuality from an exciting partner can be more than invigorating, it can be life-enhancing (see Chapter 6).

The drawbacks to choosing younger are perhaps obvious in an age-gap relationship. The younger partner may be still in a demanding career while you are either contemplating or are actually retired. This means, naturally, that they are not as available to spend or share their time as you would wish. Waiting for them to retire, depending on how far away they are from retirement, may not work as a late-life plan for you.

There may also be an economic imbalance. The later dater might be financially stable or even wealthy, whereas someone ten to fifteen years younger may have not yet arrived at that point. The later dater may also be successful in her profession or business, which may be a faraway goal for a younger partner.

The younger man may possibly resent such a situation, in which case the relationship will certainly be short term. Or, as is my experience, he may admire and be proud of the older woman's accomplishments and success. He may also not be as free of you from family commitments or demanding responsibilities. He may have an ex-wife or two plus children, family, and friends who disapprove.

Disapproval may also come from your side of the family and from friends, colleagues, or acquaintances, although a seasoned later dater should be able at this stage of life to make her own decisions about her lifestyle and relationships without bowing to pressure from others. Among them may be the partners or husbands of your girlfriends, who may also disapprove because they will assume you're trying to introduce their wives or girlfriends to the "younger man" way of life and then they will be discarded. That is, unless they themselves are younger men.

But as a sensible and independent older woman, you can take such difficulties or criticisms in stride. You have the life experience and emotional stability to cope.

However, the main drawback may be your own fears and insecurities. Never discount how deep the societal indoctrination lies within each of us. You may secretly think that what you're doing is wrong and goes against the flow of normal societal dating. Just remember that men don't think any such thing and go ahead with enthusiasm, given the opportunity. There's no valid reason women shouldn't do the same.

You may worry (or wish) that it won't last long term. That isn't to say it can't become serious and long term — quite a number of age-gap relationships do — but it's always wise to take the stance that you'll see where it goes and just enjoy the relationship to the fullest while it lasts. After all, how many other types of relationships do you know that last long term nowadays? At this stage of your life, what you most likely want is for the relationship to last as long as it is viable and pleasurable for both.

You may wonder if he'll just use you for sexual pleasure (not all bad, if you feel the same about him) then leave you high and dry. Again, this is a normal insecurity in many relationships, and there is no guarantee that he won't. On the other hand, you may be the one who ends it for any one of a wide variety of reasons.

"He'll leave me for a younger woman" is a line that is often repeated. But, when a man dates older, it's because he likes older women because they offer him so much more intellectually, sexually, and emotionally. In other words, such men are dating older women because they want to! They could date women younger or the same age, but they choose not to. He wants to date you, not someone else.

Even when men are much younger and may at some point want to marry and have a family, it's interesting how many of those having a relationship with an older woman are unwilling to leave to pursue such a situation with a younger woman. They're so enamoured of the older woman and the life they have together.

Often, the older woman has to be firm and make the decision for him to leave and start his family because it may certainly not be what she can provide or even want for her later life plan. Usually the later dater doesn't encounter such procreative problems, although whether it becomes an issue or not depends very much on the age of her younger beau.

Overall, a later dater who prefers to date younger will find it to be a more energetic, sexual, exciting, and demanding dating lifestyle that appears to suit the many women who retain their health, vitality, sexual enthusiasm, and sense of adventure into their later years. If you don't feel you fit into these categories, then it's best you find someone who shares not only your age group but also your outlook on life, love, and ageing.

One thing is for sure: if your younger date turns into a serious, long-term relationship, at least it means you won't end up his nurse.

Although it's possible he may end up as yours.

Chapter Six

You Want Me To Do What?

When entering the dating arena, it's best to know that, no matter how you feel about it, sex will raise its head, so to speak, at some point.

For most later daters, it can mean exercising their considerable sexual skills and knowledge, honed to perfection over the years. For others, who might not have been active for some time, it might be daunting, if not positively scary. The issue might be a barrier some might not want to attempt to overcome.

Which is a shame, if that's what is holding them back from a fulfilling and satisfying outlet for their passion and need to connect intimately with someone. A positive and healthy attitude about sex and sexuality can help women overcome any fears or trepidations about resuming the activity after a long dry spell.

Good sex on a regular basis is, after all, a most enjoyable bonding activity that relaxes, maintains flexibility, gives a healthy glow, helps keep you cheerful, possibly extends life, and is extremely beneficial for stable mental health and a positive outlook.

Most single men, if they're physically able and no matter what their age, have a life-long interest in sexual activity and when they enter a new relationship, this may be uppermost in their mind. Men who want to merely be a "companion" or "friend" without any sexual intimacy, while they undoubtedly exist, are few and far between. If they are willing to be just a companion or friend, it might be because they are unable to physically consummate a relationship.

Yet I am constantly surprised by the number of older single women who are adamantly searching for such partners. They are, therefore, often upset when men, after a period of being just "companions" or "friends," want to take the relationship a step further into more physical closeness. So it's wise when deciding you wish to join the later dater world, to understand that you will once more eventually enjoy sexual intimacy with a new partner.

For some women, this is a major, exciting goal, and can involve achieving sexual satisfaction for the first time in their lives; for others, it's an experimental and fascinating journey or a road full of emotional potholes to be avoided if possible; while many others can hardly wait for the physical activity to begin.

But for most later daters, the main question is not whether to have sex because they understand its place and importance in relationships, but when is the right time with someone new? And since it may have been a long time since you last dated, you might be shocked by how very different rules and attitudes about sex are today.

You may be under the impression that the dating scenario is still boy-meets-girl, which then becomes a relationship and, since it's developing well, there's a possibility of intimacy and a future together. Sorry to dash your quaint romantic dreams and fantasies, but in most cases, it simply isn't like that anymore. While in the distant past, it was relationship first, sex after, in today's dating world, it's sex first, relationship after. And it really doesn't matter the age of the male in question.

It's said that a woman knows within three minutes after she meets a man whether she is going to sleep with him. With many men, it often takes three seconds. These may be uncomfortable realities, but they're worth absorbing beforehand so you're mentally well prepared.

When?

One of the major questions connected with sexuality asked by later daters entering the dating field for the first time after a long absence is, "when is it appropriate to have sex with someone new in your life?"

Of course, how quickly — or slowly — this happens depends on what you want, the nature of the relationship, how well it is working between the two of you, whether you like and desire each other, and whether you are both emotionally ready for such intimacy.

As later daters, women are quite capable of making that decision for themselves, and yet they're often still programmed with old ideas and traditions. This can mean giving in to sexual pressure merely because that was what happened years ago. In the past, giving in was often because of the fear of losing "someone special" if you didn't agree to the proposition or were perhaps thinking it might "cement" the relationship.

As independent, savvy, intelligent, worldly older women who decide what they want — and don't want — we don't have to cave to pressure at this, or any other, stage of our life. When to have sex with someone new is your decision and yours alone.

If you still need a flexible guideline, a frequent later dater told me that she insists on at least three full dates before having sex and then only if she feels the relationship has future potential. Another said her criterion was six or more dates.

A lesson I learned early on in my later dater experiences was a simple, but harsh, one. If the relationship is about to become sexual, make sure you ask your partner for "exclusivity." This is, of course, if being exclusive is important to you and, quite frankly, it should be (more on this topic later).

It sounds simple, but at the time I made the mistake of not asking for exclusivity right from the start when a particular relationship was developing. I discovered not long after we had become intimate that he was dating, and having sex with, other women. When challenged, he stated, and I quote, "I didn't know you wanted an exclusive relationship!"

So, although it may not apply to every single older man, and I find older men can be more gentlemanly about the subject, if you don't ask for a one-on-one situation, you may very well not get it. This is especially true today, when the old dating "rules" are much more relaxed and having multiple partners is far more common.

Some single male later daters, having discovered they are in demand because they're in short supply, make hay while the sun shines and think nothing of dating many women at one time. Some women follow suit, of course, but for the most part, the female later dater prefers an exclusive sexual relationship with someone she has dated a number of times, got know better, feels some lust or desire for, and respects.

She wants it all to be reciprocated.

Sexual Etiquette

When the time comes for a closer and more intimate situation, there are a few practical factors to consider.

If either of you has your own house, condo, or apartment and there aren't any members of your family living with you, then it is easy to decide where to go. But either or both of you may have adult children or elderly, maybe ailing, parents at home, in which case other arrangements, such as a motel, a friend's place, a weekend away, might be necessary. If a cruise is suggested, usually by the man, you can be sure that he absolutely has in mind that it will include being together in the same cabin — and sex.

One thing is certain — the later dater is not usually interested in steamy trysts in the back seat of a car — too many physical contortions that will, for sure, bring on the cramps. Nothing kills desire faster.

Safe Sex

Another extremely important factor is carrying — and using — condoms. The new later dater may be unfamiliar with such items, especially if they're single after a long-term monogamous relationship. But condoms are utterly and totally essential in today's dating world.

Later daters of both sexes do not like condoms. They consider them a barrier to spontaneity and possibly to complete pleasure. But here is a sobering fact: the fastest growing demographic with STDs — sexually transmitted diseases — is the 50-plus woman.

This may shock you, but the reason is straightforward. Many older men did not grow up with the habit of using condoms, having seen them as unnecessary in a time when disease risk was minimal and dealt with easily if contracted. An old male saying was "it's like taking a bath with your overcoat on."

For a number of men, the very sight of a condom is enough to make them lose their passion as well as their erection. If this happens when matters have become steamy, the woman has to quickly decide how much she wants full sexual activity to continue with this man. Far too often she decides that she doesn't want to lose the chance of such enjoyment or doesn't want to spoil a promising situation, so she takes the risk and agrees to have sex with him without a condom.

The result, again far too often, is that she gets an STD because the man may be sexually active with other women as well, maybe all of them making exactly the same decision.

And it's no good saying you're absolutely certain you're the only one. You can't be 100 percent sure unless you're a couple living together 24/7. So a major sexual rule of today is always insist on safe sex — or no sex. It's the only way to avoid serious health repercussions.

But if you feel you may have contracted something during a sexual encounter, check immediately with your doctor or a clinic.

Body Image

Another major factor about having sex at a later age, perhaps more for women than for men, is a personal issue of their own body image. Despite the fact that women are most likely dating, or wanting to date, a man who is of similar age or older, they feel self-conscious about life's wear and tear on their shape and figure.

Yet the truth is, a man is certainly not expecting, or even wanting, to see a woman of his own age or similar with a body of a 20-year-old model. This isn't to say that the later dater hasn't worked hard to be trim, fit, and in excellent shape for her age group, it's just that many older women worry unnecessarily about the first time they undress for sex with someone new.

Now, while I have always maintained that having sex for the first time in candlelight is one wonderful way of making it all seem magical, it's my experience that with most men, the first sexual experience with someone new they desire is stimulating and exciting enough. In other words, they aren't concerning themselves at that moment with a woman's figure faults but with the anticipated consummation of their lust and passion.

And if the sex is as good and exciting as they expect it will be, and in turn the woman has shown equal enthusiasm (very important), when the action is over, the last thought in their mind is a critique of your body. A satisfied mind and body does not look for fault.

If that fails to convince, then a few tips may help.

- If it's been a long time since you were sexually active and you feel you've lost touch with what to do and how to do it, read a quality book on sex for ideas, helpful tips, and good advice.

- Wear your best underwear for the encounter and, if all you have is practical, plain, beige, built-for-comfort pants and bras, shop for items that are more colourful and more attractive, in a flattering, sexy design. Feeling sexy and confident underneath your clothes helps you feel the same outside them.

- Invest in a lovely robe that may be a far cry from your warm, woolly, everyday standby. It will give you the same feeling as the pretty underwear and be most useful for that quick wrap-up afterwards.

- Set the scene, if possible, with candlelight, glasses of wine, soft music, fresh sheets (if in your bedroom). Perhaps more seductive than practical, it's obviously not always possible to set a scene when passion arises suddenly or you're not in your own home.

- If vaginal dryness is a concern, either apply some lubricant well before an expected sexual encounter or keep a small bottle or tube of it where you can reach it easily.

- Realize that your male partner may have very similar worries himself about his body, his performance, and your pleasure.

- Relax and enjoy yourself. This is perhaps the biggest and best tip of all. An anxious and nervous partner can dissipate passion both in you and in your companion and spoil a lovely moment.

The action

While a later dater may have been the most athletic, active, imaginative contortionist in the style of the Kama Sutra in her past sexual activities, it's possible such wild activity no longer quite works for her nor does it bring extra pleasure. In other words, as we age, our bodies are not quite as limber and, when we're confronted with putting our extremities into odd sexual positions, nasty cramps and other strains can set in. This can be embarrassing and can certainly damper passion. It can be unpleasant and painful the next day too.

The good news is that men of your own age or older are usually at exactly the same stage, maybe more so, unless they're still active triathletes or tennis players. But even for the fittest of us, it may just be that as we age, we find that a gentler, more basic approach to sex is more satisfying and comforting than wild contortions.

Cuddling, caressing, and massaging with oils may constitute a wonderful part of foreplay in mature relationships, while plenty of skilled oral sex (for both parties) can provide excitement and satisfaction. It is good to note (although I'm certain the later dater learned this a long time ago and may be very skilled in this area) that oral sex is a pleasure very high indeed on the sexual list of men of all ages.

It's also possible that our sexual horizons, and those of our partner, have expanded to other areas, which may include fantasy sex, dressing up, and the use of sex toys and aids. Other fetishes, such as an exploration of bondage or sado-masochism, may not appeal to the majority of women. As recent bestseller lists indicate, however, many women are quite fond of erotic novels that include such activities and may encourage the soft side of bondage, for instance, in lovemaking. But, as with all sexual activity, if the activity doesn't appeal or even disturbs you, make sure you state your views firmly before the activity begins (if you know, that is).

As most later daters already know very well, no one should ever be coerced into doing anything they don't want to do. Sex should always be a pleasure for both people.

Disabilities, illness, and impotency

It's perhaps not the most uplifting way to talk about the joy of sex for the later dater, but being practical and informed helps in a number of situations, including sexuality, when dating as an older person.

There will occasionally be some physical difficulties to surmount with aging partners, but you can handle most well with open communication and caring while still having a good sexual connection. A major setback with many men as they age can be erection problems, or ED (erectile dysfunction). This can be mild or severe and temporary or permanent. And many female later daters, unfortunately, may not be told about their potential partner's problem for a while. Many men resist divulging such very personal information even when there are a lengthy number of excellent dates and it is obvious at some point that intimacy will be expected.

Why, you may ask, would a man keep such highly relevant and important information from a potential relationship? My theory, and I want to make it clear that it is just my own theory from some experiences, is that the man wishes to find out the kind of woman you are. He wants to ascertain whether or not you're a woman who is sexual and therefore requires the full sex act or one who might be content with far less or possibly no penetration at all.

If you are a sexy, sensual woman who undoubtedly has expectations of a full sexual encounter, then he has to decide between two actions. Should he tell you and see your obvious disappointment and deal with the possibility that you may walk away or should he keep it from you (a risky move)?

Yet the way some men deal with it is just that. They keep the information secret, then suddenly dump the woman for no obvious reason before a sexual encounter can take place. Heartless, but not uncommon.

The woman is left wondering what went wrong and, more often than not, perhaps blames herself for the failure of what appeared to be a good, budding relationship.

The kind, considerate, and honest way is for men to state from the beginning that there is a problem and leave it to you to decide if you wish to stay or go. But, to be fair, it's likely a very difficult and embarrassing subject for both parties and far too often avoided until it's too late.

It happened to me. I should have used my experience and known better but didn't because I was so excited about the new relationship. Lesson learned.

My advice is, if you think there may be a problem, don't ask directly whether he has ED or not (a fast way to embarrass a man and make him disappear), but listen to him when he talks about his health. If he's had a heart attack or heart surgery, for instance, one way to learn more is to enquire about the medications he's taking. Then check with someone knowledgeable, such as a healthcare provider or pharmacist, to see if those medications can cause impotence (most of them do). You'll get some idea of what to expect.

Prostate problems (and certainly surgical prostate removal) may also be a sign of considerable difficulty or non-existent ability. As well, some medications for angina, diabetes, depression, blood pressure, strokes, epilepsy, lowering cholesterol, ulcers, and suppressing acid can cause erection problems.

Natural aging processes can often mean a less powerful erection, but that doesn't necessarily have to be a problem because most men know what gives them the best erection, usually plenty of direct friction.

The famous anti-impotence pill, Viagra, may be for many older men the must-have accessory if they're single and dating, and also the answer to their fears. However, many medications cannot be safely combined with Viagra, and taking the drug also requires advance planning, because it takes time to take effect. Other drugs, such as Cialis and Levitra, have a longer-lasting effect and may be more suitable. Viagra was designed to increase sexual response in men with impotence problems and is not necessarily a blanket solution for men experiencing performance anxiety or natural aging changes. Men should consult with a doctor or healthcare provider before taking Viagra or any other such drug.

Despite considerable efforts by the pharmaceutical companies to discover a concoction to improve sexual desire in women, we all know there's no better drug to ensure complete satisfaction than a loving, considerate, passionate, sexually-skilled partner we desire.

Arthritis

Arthritis difficulties, often experienced by both older men and women, can affect movement during sex, with pain being an unpleasant drawback to active sex. But honest communication about it between partners is the answer — as it is with everything, of course — and will help the other partner understand what can be achieved and what cannot. A warm bath before sex or taking medication specifically for relief of arthritis can both help you relax and make you relatively pain-free for a while. Using cushions or pillows for comfort and support during intercourse will also be helpful.

Disability

It's a myth that people living with disabilities are not or cannot be sexual. And it's a myth that sex is bad for people who have had strokes. The medical profession says sex is, in moderation, actually helpful to their recovery.

If either you or your date has a disability, while it may be difficult initially for the partner to adjust or look beyond the actual disability, it certainly doesn't need to mean that a great relationship, including sex, can't happen.

Society has a very disturbing idea that disabled people live a life that's not worth living, that those living with disabilities are somehow a burden. It's an attitude that is absolutely offensive and completely erroneous.

Many disabled people lead full, active, and productive lives and many are wonderful friends, partners, and lovers. Sex experienced by those with a disability may be somewhat different in approach and accomplishment from sex experienced by the non-disabled, but many with disabilities enjoy a satisfying sex life.

Again, for many people with disabilities, the best approach to sexuality is through open and honest discussion of sex and their disability, finding pain-free and discomfort-free ways that work for them, and explaining what is possible and not possible. Successful sex involves being adaptive and imaginative and sometimes using sexual toys and aids.

You can find a number of excellent sources regarding disability and sex on the Internet as well as support groups for those wishing to learn more.

Everyone wants to be cherished and loved, and sexual intimacy with a loving partner is a beneficial and pleasurable experience that is surely a basic human right.

The happiest people are undoubtedly those who enjoy regular sexual activity with someone they care about and who cares for them

Chapter Seven

Everyone's a Critic

The old saying "all the world loves a lover" was surely aimed at the younger generation. Most single older women who are thinking of dating or are already actively doing so are only too aware that it often isn't true for them. It could almost be said that the whole world is suspicious of, doesn't understand, sneers at, or is fearful of women of over 50 who are dating and looking for another relationship.

Despite changing times, more awareness, and relaxed sexual and social attitudes towards alternative relationships, people still seem to be shocked by the mature single woman actively seeking another partner. This is, of course, in contrast to society's complete acceptance of older single men doing the same thing.

The double standard is because the female later dater is a completely new social phenomenon, totally unknown in past decades. In the past, once a woman was widowed or divorced in mid or late life, or even if she remained single, she was on the periphery and almost ostracized from society. She was expected to be invisible, in the background, and fulfill her role as elder wise woman, a mother, grandmother, or caregiver, none of which involved forming a close, personal relationship with a male, especially not a relationship that might be — oh, horrors! — sexual!

I have, in previous chapters, given some of the reasons why society is unable to dig itself out of the pit of ancient prejudices and fears about older women. One of the major reasons is that, with a few exceptions, older women had never before been considered to be sexual, sensual, desirable, or even particularly valuable to society, despite obvious indications of the opposite in today's vibrant older generation of women.

So it's wise to expect and be prepared for a reaction from various directions in the later dater's life, and these reactions may not always be supportive.

While a number of people close to the later dater might be very encouraging, negativity might come from the later dater's family, friends, co-workers, employees, and social group, or from society in general.

Family

The prominent area of criticism and condemnation usually comes from the later dater's immediate family. Despite the fact that her children are most likely to be adults, they are more than likely to resist and perhaps resent their mother entering the dating arena, especially if it's for the first time since she was young and single.

The most enlightened ones will be worried about her emotional ability to withstand contemporary dating pressures or even fearful for her safety. But the basis of all the angst is simple. Children don't like their mother dating. It messes with their ingrained concept of "mother as Madonna" or, at least, as their personal rock who will always be there to nurture and protect them.

They may also still be attached to their father, if their parents are divorced, and see any male in their mother's life to be an intruder, usurper or, for the more mercenary ones, a divider of future inheritance spoils.

If their father has passed, they may be protective of his memory and mired in the traditional idea that with his passing, their mother's life as a social and sexual being ended.

If their father is still around and involved with them, they will most certainly tell him about their mother's activities, often embellishing with critical details (real or imagined) that will make him wince and feel uncomfortable.

It's a volatile and difficult minefield, both for the woman and for any man she chooses to bring into her life and introduce to her children.

The answer for the later dater is to initially be discreet about her dating activity, then slowly introduce the idea to her children so that they have time to get used to the idea.

The best way, of course, is to sit them down and discuss the situation openly and honestly with them. Listen graciously to their concerns and encourage them to talk about their feelings about it all while firmly pointing out that since you are now a single person, you're entitled to a life of your own, reminding them that you love them very much.

I've always strongly believed that if you love someone, you want them to be happy. It's a valid point to make to truculent offspring if matters get problematic.

Once it has been fully discussed without rancour (hopefully without any of them — or you — flouncing out of the room in anger and disgust), you can approach the subject of their meeting your date (or dates). This can perhaps take the form of a casual dinner out together, a supper at home, or just having your date for a drink at home first when he comes to collect you for an evening out.

Don't be hurt or surprised if one or more of your children makes excuses and doesn't attend or even refuses to be there. The meeting of mother's new man often takes considerable time to adjust to.

It's best however, not to make "meeting the family" turn into a revolving door of ever-changing men, even if you've discovered that dating is working only too successfully for you and you have a number of exciting prospects. If this is your scenario, then lucky you! But be selective and cautious when deciding which ones to introduce to your offspring.

Of course, it's possible (and the best situation) that your child or children may also be dating and may be quite comfortable with you doing the same. Besides, they might give you some good tips.

But your adult children may not be the only family obstacle to your new social life. You might also have elderly parents who could be shocked that you're actually "stepping out" at this time of your life. Again, much of the above advice for children applies to your parents whose societal ideas, although from the distant past, may hopefully have mellowed through the years and made them more accepting of change.

If not, the gentle but firm approach of providing basic information plus reiterating your entitlement to a life is best. If you feel it will only cause upset and trauma, then keep your dating life private.

As for uncles, aunts, nephews, and nieces, it's none of their business. They will, however, make it their business if you're dating someone they know. And they'll let you know their opinion.

Friends

Most later daters will find that their friends divide into four camps —
those who are dating, those who aren't but would like to, those who are
horrified (or terrified) at the very idea, and those who are married.

The ones who are dating are obviously the easiest friends to deal with
and have around because you can swap experiences and ideas with them
(good and bad) because they're undoubtedly going through the same
situations. They will, of course, want to know every detail of how you met
your latest date and also frequently ask how the relationship is going and
how he treats you. This can be a caring query or one by which they're
checking out the situation, thinking, if it's going badly for you, maybe he's
worth chasing for themselves

Those who aren't dating but would like to will be divided among the
supportive, envious, and secretly jealous. It will depend on your friendship
and their view of their own prospects whether discussions on your dating
activities are fun or plain awkward. With luck, your efforts may encourage
those friends to jump in themselves and you can share the joys and pitfalls of
later dating.

Your friends who are terrified or, worse, horrified at the very idea
should be spared the details of your newfound activity unless, of course, you

love to "stir the pot" and regale them with exciting stories of fancy meals, travel, and hot nights you've enjoyed — if you have…

Married friends will be interested in your activities and only too ready to give you advice. Some of them will be more than envious of your single freedom (and possibly your active sex life, if you have one) and may offer criticism perhaps tinged with (or overwhelmed by) jealousy. Their husbands will either be amused, intrigued, completely disinterested in your dating life, or very nervous that you could be making their wife restless with a longing to be single again. They will either cheer you on or try to discourage their wife from spending too much time in your company. You will rarely be invited to their dinner parties because not only does a single person looking for a relationship throw off their nice, even numbers, but you also might be considered a threat to their other married female friends. Don't fret if this happens. You have a new life, and their dinner parties were probably excruciatingly boring anyway.

Colleagues, employees, or boss

It's very difficult to keep your private life from the people you work with every day, so be assured that they will find out soon enough —

especially if the man you're dating happens to also be a colleague — or your boss.

Dating your boss is a difficult path to choose. While some co-workers may feel who you're dating is nobody's business, others will react badly because they will maybe see the relationship as a threat to their own ambitions within the company and think that you'll be shown extra favour.

In my experience of dating a boss, it's exactly the opposite. The boss, no matter how much he adores you, will probably deliberately treat you more harshly and with less consideration than other colleagues just to prove to them that he's not showing any special favouritism toward you. Your career may not advance because of it.

My advice is to keep your head down and keep your mouth shut, especially if there might be company rules about management and subordinates being romantically involved. And don't react to any pointed barbs and comments from work colleagues. Just smile enigmatically.

If you're the boss or company owner and you're dating an employee, it can be an even touchier subject for the rest of your company. The same comments as above apply with regard to how employees and other personnel will react.

The best advice for both situations is to seek and form relationships outside of your business or work field. It's easier said than done, though, when so many of us spend most of our time in the workplace or in our business and often form close relationships there over time.

One of the joys of getting older is that retirement releases you from all the restrictions and rules of the workplace and, particularly, who you can date!

Exes — his and yours

The most difficult scenario is if you (or your new partner) still have an ex hovering who hasn't yet moved on to dating. Jealousy and misguided possessiveness may rise. Many a relationship has foundered on the endless intrusive presence of a bitter ex-partner, and it can produce a toxic situation that stresses both of you.

Communication between you and your new partner, tempered with as much understanding and tolerance as you can muster, is key, particularly if there are children, young or adult, involved.

If you're widowed, this difficulty doesn't arise, of course, although I have heard painful stories where adult daughters in particular take over their widowed father's lives as surrogate mother/wife and bitterly oppose the intrusion of another woman into their father's life. Stories of the lengths they will go to to keep a woman out of his life can be legendary and, to my mind, show they are not only very lacking in love and kindness toward their parent, but are more into keeping a tight hold onto what they consider theirs, usually property or money. It can be a rough and stressful road and perhaps one to be avoided, if possible.

Another problem in widowed life is perhaps the continuing revered devotion of a partner towards their late wife/husband. While this is obviously a human reaction to the loss of someone very special, it can be taken to extremes, for example, the surviving spouse might keep their dead partner's clothes in the closets, have numerous photos throughout the house, and insist on keeping everything in the household exactly the same as it was when the spouse was alive. This can be uncomfortable and even creepy if you spend any length of time together in the person's home. Desire dies when you feel there's an overwhelming atmosphere of someone else's presence, even if they've passed on.

If gentle, caring persuasion doesn't convince the widowed person to put the past behind them and adjust now they have started a new relationship and possibly a new future, it might be wise to reconsider the relationship and find someone else. The eternal devotion and dedication to keeping the memory of their past spouse alive may be too ingrained and too much to overcome at this stage of their life

As a later dater you should be aware of keeping your past in the past, no matter what the circumstance, but always with the understanding between you and your new relationship that, if you were happily married and he has passed, he would always have a piece of your heart and vice versa.

Bitter divorces or broken relationships are always best left behind. Look forward, not back. Bitterness and anger only destroy the person who has these feelings festering in them and can certainly ruin any potential happiness when one is looking for a new relationship. And no one new in your life wants to hear the unpleasant details because it means you're still living in the past and not looking for a totally fresh start.

Chapter Eight

Putting Your Best Face Forward

No matter how strong, independent, and liberated women become, most (okay, all) are dissatisfied with at least one aspect of their appearance (okay, sometimes a lot of aspects). This dissatisfaction often comes to a peak when she's dating later in life and looking for a new relationship.

The later dater, however, is different from previous generations of women. She is proactive and knows how to cope. She's well aware that looking fresh and vital helps her feel good, and that feeling good produces self-confidence, that magical quality so essential as we age and which can slip away so quickly when we think we don't look or feel our best.

The later dater is also practical and business savvy. She knows it's a competitive world, not only in a business environment but also in the dating market.

Decades ago, diamonds may have been considered a girl's best friend. In today's youth-oriented and highly competitive world, a far better investment is the phone number of the best cosmetic surgeon and anti-aging physician in town. Once considered a vanity, cosmetic surgery and aesthetic enhancement is a now major growth industry and well accepted by society.

The taboo of self-enhancement is gone. Women consider it an investment in themselves and acknowledge it as not only a way to improve on nature, but also a recognized path to increased self-confidence.

Fortunately, the medical industry has advanced to the point where many aesthetic enhancements that will give the later dater an "appearance edge" and self-confidence are non-surgical and are minimally invasive, meaning they're fast and there is little or no down time for recovery, perfect for today's hectic lifestyles.

Starting out

If you feel strongly that cosmetic surgery or non-surgical enhancements can help your confidence and renew your vitality, then it's right for you. People for sure will ask you, or wonder aloud, why you'd put yourself through such a thing and perhaps try to persuade you not to go ahead. But most women who consider such an option know what they want and are rarely dissuaded.

The first step is to find a reputable aesthetic surgeon or enhancement physician that you like and with whom you feel comfortable. It's also vital that he or she understand exactly what you want to achieve. Your goals and needs must be realistic and achievable.

One of the best ways to find a good aesthetic surgeon is to talk to women who have had cosmetic surgery or cosmetic enhancement procedures. This can be somewhat difficult if they want you to believe that they look fantastic because (a) they've just returned from a long vacation, (b) are working out more, (c) are on a diet, or (d) have just landed a hot relationship. If you can't find any women who will admit to having had work done, then call your local plastic surgery association and get the names of qualified aesthetic plastic surgeons in your area.

Visit at least three before making a decision. These days, the later dater can spend useful time researching online the procedure options, risks, recovery, and good physicians. Like online dating, a lot of fact gathering can be at your fingertips in the comfort of your own home.

Be aware that all major cosmetic surgery has health risks, involves sedation or general anesthesia, and will require three to four weeks of recovery (and much longer for full healing).

For the neophyte, the place to start is with non-surgical enhancements. Like any rejuvenating project, cosmetic surgery is best approached by doing one part at a time. Most modern plastic surgery techniques are minimally invasive and can often be performed under local anesthesia with less risk and a shorter recovery period than in the past.

Here are some of the newer techniques available from top surgeons today.

A.   Non-surgical aesthetic enhancement options

If the thought of what has always been known as "going under the knife" makes you pale, there are new, exciting, and amazing anti-aging alternatives available that don't require a scalpel.

Scientists already know how to decipher the genetic code. They are also able to test the level of a person's DNA damage and then repair it. Analytical tests like these, tests that can lead to the repair of our aging cells, will mean that, eventually, it will be possible to manipulate a person's DNA to optimize his or her anti-aging abilities. People will live far longer — and far healthier — and not suffer the current debilitating damage that ages them.

In an Orwellian sense, these new genetic and biomedical advances mean that the future of cosmetic surgery may well be no surgery at all. We just won't age! (A happy thought!)

Anti-aging products and supplements

These offer the least invasive way to look and feel good and combat aging from the inside out. One of the most popular methods of keeping aging at bay, (especially the effects of menopause), is hormone therapy.

Hormone therapy can help invigorate a slowing system and keep skin and hair youthful. It can also reduce menopausal symptoms such as hot flashes and irritability, and increase vaginal lubrication. It's important for the later dater to work with an experienced anti-aging physician because hormonal manipulation must be balanced against any gynecological risks.

For those who prefer a more holistic approach, taking naturally occurring substances and nutraceuticals can augment the body's natural release of hormones.

For the latest in non-invasive, anti-aging techniques, consult a physician who specializes in anti-aging medicine. For more information, search under "anti-aging" on the Internet. Two excellent sites are the Longevity Institute International and the American Academy of Anti-Aging Medicine www.longevity-institute.com and www.worldhealth.net.a4m/html.

Laser treatment, skin care, and non-surgical cosmetic enhancement services

No matter how much you exercise, how well you eat, and how many supplements you take, the odd blemish or age spot will still crop up from time to time, regardless of your age. Those blemishes that don't respond to surface creams and potions, such as spider veins, brown spots, large pores, and wrinkles, can be dealt with permanently by several methods.

Most later daters experience the 3Ds of aging, namely, deflation, descent, and deterioration, all of which can be successfully treated with the techniques outlined below. (Of course, I prefer my own 3Ds of aging — desire, dancing, and delight — but these are undoubtedly enhanced when you're looking and feeling splendid.

Botox and soft-tissue fillers

Botox and soft-tissue fillers are the most common techniques used in anti-aging today. Botox relaxes the muscles of facial expression that cause frown lines, worry lines, and crows' feet that can add years or a sense of "danger" to the mature face. Soft tissue fillers, injected in areas of deflation and grooves, now come in all manners and varieties, many of which will last you one or two years.

When considering these procedures, search for a fully qualified, talented injector who will work with your face like an artist, so that you don't end up with the dreaded "filler face." Done well, Botox and fillers can take five to seven years off the age of a mature woman, naturally and effectively. Most practitioners will combine Botox and fillers with light-, laser-, and energy-based skin treatments, outlined next.

IPL, laser, and FotoFacial treatment

Intense pulsed light (IPL), laser, and FotoFacial treatments are non-invasive, outpatient methods for minimizing spider veins, rosacea, brown spots, and age spots. FotoFacial therapy has no down time and no recovery time, and makeup can be applied immediately afterwards — a sort of medical takeout system for those on the run!

Radiofrequency and ultrasound tightening

Radiofrequency (RF) devices emit electrical current and are good at skin tightening as well as wrinkle and pore reduction. Several treatments over several weeks and ongoing maintenance post-procedure are usually required. RF devices (such as Thermage, FIRM, Accent Excelis, and others) are reasonably affordable and will tighten moderately lax jawlines, necks, and lower lids.

New ultrasound devices, such as Ulthera, can also be used alone or in combination with radiofrequency in-office treatments to tighten lax brow, face, and neck tissues.

Fractional laser and RF resurfacing techniques

New fractional laser and RF devices have become very popular, are highly advanced, and are acknowledged as the best answer to selectively remove layers of wrinkled and rough skin. Fractional lasers and RF devices (Fraxel, eMatrix, Fractora) work by creating a thermal injury in part of the skin and then leaving some adjacent skin intact to facilitate rapid wound healing.

For the later dater, this fractional approach is important, because you get the wrinkle reduction and skin enhancement of the old-fashioned, full-face, CO_2 laser resurfacing but with very little in the way of side effects. This allows new skin to regenerate and grow. The actual process is fast, and recovery times can be a weekend or several days, depending upon the energies used.

Chemical peels, microdermabrasion, and medical skincare

Combinations of light, RF, and fractional lasers together with physician-delivered chemical peels, microdermabrasion, and medical skincare afterwards are a good method of protecting your in-office investments.

Aesthetic physicians will use alpha or beta hydroxyl acids, or glycolic acid to remove several layers of skin through the application of chemical acids. A light peel results in a few days of redness and flaking; deeper peels using phenol or trichloracetic acid (TCA) require two or three weeks of recovery.

Medical microdermabrasion uses either tiny crystals or ultrasonic energy to basically scour away the skin's top surface, removing shallow wrinkles, lip lines, and small scars. Physician-strength skincare products will help keep the skin bright and smooth.

Laser hair removal

Unwanted post-menopausal facial hair and extra body hair may present a problem for the woman who would prefer smooth, hair-free skin. If you're tired of waxing, shaving, and plucking, try laser hair-removal techniques to get rid of superfluous hair. In-office, physician-strength laser hair systems (such as LightSheer and Elite) are fast and affordable methods of permanently reducing hair from the upper lip, chin, bikini line, and more.

Varicose vein removal

Gone are the painful leg-vein-stripping procedures of yesteryear. The newest techniques are minimally invasive and use ultrasound technology to diagnose where the deep veins are leaking — one cause of enlarged and varicose veins. Once these leaky veins are identified, tiny laser or RF catheters are inserted to emit either a laser wavelength or a radio frequency to close off the leak. Once the large varicose veins have been closed, the superficial spider veins are removed with lasers or traditional sclerotherapy.

Cellulite and stretch marks

Newer radiofrequency and ultrasound devices have replaced body wraps and endermologic techniques for the long-term reduction in the appearance of cellulite. These devices are successful in combating the dreaded orange-peel look of skin, usually on the buttocks and thighs.

New fractional lasers and radiofrequency devices are also effective when applied to minimize stretch marks.

Home light-based treatments

There has been an explosion in approved home-based laser, light, and RF devices, although these techniques are not nearly as successful as the in-office procedures. Once you've completed a series of laser hair removal, fractional skin resurfacing, or skin tightening through a physician, however, you can find many now-affordable home laser- and light-based treatments for maintaining the improvements (Silk'n, Flash and Go, Tria, and no!no! for keeping the hair away; FaceFx for tightening the skin; and ClearFx for maintaining clear skin).

More medical-grade skincare products

Anti-aging doctors now have an arsenal of active, topical, skin products to keep the skin healthy, clear, and youthful. These physician-prescribed products (Obagi, SkinCeuticals, Skinmedica, etc.) have more potency than over-the-counter creams and lotions. Some of the newest and most effective are derivatives of vitamin A (such as Retinol and Retin A); derivatives of vitamin C; hydroquinone and kogic acid to tighten and brighten skin; co-enzyme Q10 L; and bioactive and proven serums and acid lotions to diminish skin damage and promote collagen production. These products can cause untoward side effects, however, and should be used only after consultation with your doctor.

All the information above is intentionally brief. It is offered only as a guideline to some of the current advances in anti-aging and rejuvenation. Always first consult a doctor, cosmetic plastic surgeon, or anti-aging specialist

B.   Cosmetic plastic surgery options

Although non-surgical options can do a great job providing rejuvenation, for serious aging concerns, modern plastic surgery techniques offer the most complete and long-term correction and restoration.

Face and neck

The later dater may spend many hours keeping her body toned, fit, and youthful, and she will certainly want her face to match.

These days, the upper two-thirds of the face can be rejuvenated and elevated endoscopically, eliminating the need for large incisions. Tiny telescopes are used to reposition droopy brows, cheeks, and mid-face areas; lift the corners of mouths; and eliminate smile lines. Even those dreaded jowls can get a partial pick-me-up with this method. The combination of appropriate (not ridiculous) volumization using fat grafting or long-term fillers and with endoscopic lifts can provide a natural result.

Eyes

The contemporary approach to eye surgery is to preserve and reposition fat, preventing the hollowed-out look that was once so common. Lower lid surgery can now be done behind the eye and inside the lower lid. Fat bags are gone and the lower lid is left scarless.

Nose

As women age, the tip of the nose can droop or appear bulbous. A rhinoplasty, or soft tissue tip "nose job" will reposition it to balance the bridge and look more youthful.

Lips

Full, sensual lips are a definite sign of youth. Micro fat transplantation and the newer injectable fillers can create fuller lips that look both younger and natural.

Neck

Wrinkly necks can be smoothed by lifting and tightening the facial muscles (along with the loose skin) and, together with fractional lasers, can give a longer-lasting and more effective lift to the sworn enemy of the mature women — the "turkey neck."

Breasts

In today's society, whether or not we agree, full, firm breasts are still viewed as desirable by both men and women. There are many theories as to why, but the reasons are not important. What is important is that a woman is happy with hers.

Augmentation is still very popular and can now be carried out endoscopically (no scarring). Implants are filled with salt water or the more popular cohesive gel ("gummy bear implant") that holds the shape of the breast. These days, women can also choose the shape, teardrop or round. Breast lifting (without augmentation) can rejuvenate the breasts by removing excess skin and maintaining the same breast volume in a perkier position.

The modern cosmetic plastic surgeon will use high-tech, preoperative 3D-imaging devices to show you your breast size and shape before you commit to buying.

Stomach

The traditional tummy tuck is still the method of choice for rejuvenating an aging stomach. The tummy tuck can remove loose skin, tighten loose muscles, and erase unattractive stretch marks. An endoscopic tummy tuck tightens and flattens an untoned, bulging stomach. Since no skin is removed during the procedure, healthy, non-damaged skin is a must. Often, modern liposuction techniques, such as SmartLipo or BodyTite, can be combined with the tummy tuck to shrink fat, tighten skin, and minimize the size of the tummy-tuck scar.

Body sculpting with new energy-assisted liposuction devices

While not a solution for those looking to lose a lot of weight, modern liposuction techniques can be used to sculpt body contours.

As a woman ages, unwanted body fat can appear on the upper arms, neck, outer and inner thighs, hips and waist, abdomen, inner knees, and buttocks. This fat can be removed by the insertion of a cannula — a metallic reed-like tube that draws out fat. Microcannulas that emit a laser (SmartLipo) or electrical current (BodyTite) can melt the fat prior to removal to help minimize trauma and injury and optimize contraction. An

126

anaesthetic solution is often injected into the fat to plump it up before removal to minimize bleeding and bruising.

A new advancement involves the use of ultrasound energy to liquefy the fat, making it easier to remove.

Artificial implants are also gaining in popularity among those looking for a fuller, more youthful contour to their facial cheeks and a fuller, rounder profile to their buttocks.

All the information above is intentionally brief. It is offered only as a guideline to some of the current advances in anti-aging and rejuvenation.
Always consult a doctor, cosmetic plastic surgeon, or anti-aging specialist before using any new product.

Cosmetic surgery and anti-aging consultant:

Dr. R. Stephen Mulholland, M.D.,
SpaMedica Cosmetic Surgery and Infinite Vitality Clinic,

66 Avenue Road, Suite 4,
Toronto, Ontario,
M5R 3N8,
Canada
www.spamedica.com

Chapter Nine

Togetherness

Although this is a book of helpful advice for female Boomers and beyond on getting proactive and finding a relationship, it surely wouldn't be complete without a chapter on what happens after you actually find that good relationship.

You've finally met him and life has lit up again for you. It's once more brimming with love, laughter, hugs, cuddles, kisses, and perhaps some satisfying sex. He feels the same, and you may now be serious about being a "together" couple. The future shines brightly.

What happens now? Which direction should you go? What plans should you make? What decisions should you make about marriage, co-habiting, separate homes, finances, and so on? Or should you just roll along at an easy pace while making no decisions at all regarding a future?

There's no question that many later daters prefer the latter, even when they form another exciting and stable relationship. They may think that they are set in their ways and don't feel they can tolerate living in close proximity to someone else after being alone for so long.

Being single may, for some people, be a lonely and occasionally desperate condition, but for others it may mean that they truly enjoy having plenty of personal space, making their own decisions about everything, and not compromising their way of life for anyone. For many of those singles, it can be hard at this stage of their life to change from ruling their own roost to sharing it all with someone else.

Those who have been previously married or in a live-in relationship are only too aware of the compromises that must be made in such an up-close-and-personal arrangement. Others feel that it's well worth giving up personal space and a private life to have the love, support, comfort, and companionship of someone special.

So, if the new relationship turns serious and there's an obvious leaning by both of you to make it a permanent arrangement, how will it work and what are the pros and cons of the various arrangements?

Separate homes

One of the biggest trends for later daters who become serious about each other and want to stay as a couple is to not get married or even move in together. They decide to keep their own homes and take turns staying at each other's places, whether overnight or for a short or long time.

The benefits of this arrangement are that you still have your independence, you still own or rent your own home, and your life and personal space remains intact.

This arrangement works well for those who travel a lot, have family living at home, have a deep personal attachment to their home, or have pets they don't want to uproot or that may not be acceptable to their new partner. It also works for those who have, for instance, a very different sleeping or daily schedule from each other that doesn't mesh well in a live-in situation, yet they want to maintain as close a relationship as possible.

Many couples resolve such difficulties by having homes close to each other, perhaps in the same condo or apartment building, on the same street, or in the same area. It's closeness without encroachment. I have even met the occasional very independent older married couple who live in this manner, and they say they sincerely find such a situation most satisfactory at this time of their life.

The drawback of living apart is that your lives, while intertwined, may not flourish as well as if you were living together.

Although, at times, living together, whether married or otherwise, can undoubtedly be stressful, experts will tell you that deeper bonds are formed between those who do live together than between those who choose to live apart. In other words, despite marital and co-habiting breakup statistics, there's still a better chance of a relationship lasting and being harmonious when partners live as one than when they live divided.

There's also the trust issue.

Having a good relationship with someone who lives in another place, has another life, and shares only a portion of it with you can be unsettling at times. It's especially unsettling for those who have, in the past, encountered trust issues as a result of a cheating partner.

Although by the time we're a later dater, there's an element of acceptance about people's weaknesses and failings, perhaps born of experience, there's no question that, for women (of all ages), cheating by their partner is still the ultimate betrayal. This isn't to say that the way to avoid it is to make sure you're with your partner 24/7 or insist on knowing where they are all the time. That smacks of paranoia and is very unattractive. For most people, this is impossible to live or deal with, especially if based on jealousy and possessiveness.

There is little that can be done about a situation (except end it) when one partner doesn't trust the other to remain faithful to the relationship, even though that partner may be blameless and even devoted. It will, of course, become a painful and divisive subject, whether a couple lives together or not. It's sensible at any age not to be so blinded by the need for a partner or by overwhelming love (or lust!) that you don't recognize the signs of a controller or one dominated by jealousy and possessiveness.

When living in separate homes, a few couples adopt the concept of an "open" relationship, in which they mutually agree that each partner can have relationships with other people while remaining "together." The pitfalls of such an arrangement, even though mutually agreeable, are obvious to any later dater with even a modicum of experience in human nature. It takes a very easygoing, even Bohemian outlook on life to agree to share the partner you love with other people emotionally and sexually without feelings and emotions taking over (yours or theirs). Open relationships, in my experience, sometimes work for a period of time when agreed to between two very grounded, independent, and self-confident people. However, most of them do not stand the test of time. And isn't the purpose of searching for a partner for the latter part of your life all about loving and cherishing each other and living life to the fullest together?

Marriage or cohabitation?

Just mentioning the "M" word may cause panic and heart palpitations to some later daters who have vowed vehemently "never again" after an unpleasant marital experience (or experiences) in the past.

As a multiple marry-er myself, I should have learned my lesson long ago. After all, most of the marriages took all or nearly all of my money. But, hey, I've always been in love with love and felt it would overcome everything. It didn't.

Why did I keep marrying then? Why not cohabit? Good question, but it's only in recent decades that cohabiting has gained acceptance, and I always found (perhaps against the general view) that men prefer to be married. More security? More control? More personal care? More easily accessible sex?

There's no question that co-habiting is on the rise with today's couples of all ages. In fact, people in their early 60s are entering common-law relationships at the most rapid rate of all the age categories. That's because it makes sense perhaps that, as a mature couple, such an arrangement might be the simplest answer.

But the choice is more complex emotionally than it appears. Certainly there can be deep bonds forged when cohabiting, and I have known a number of couples who have spent their entire relationship lives unmarried and living together very happily.

However, I have occasionally found that even with such couples, often one of them, deep down, would prefer marriage and can eventually be resentful and bitter that the other partner refuses a marital union.

Cohabiting couples may ask why anyone would bother with marriage these days, when living together is so socially acceptable and common.

And perhaps, there's the answer. Cohabitation is an "arrangement," whether mutually agreeable or not, whereas marriage is a legally binding agreement that announces proudly to the world that the union is intended to be permanent and will not be set aside, no matter what. Or at least that's the idea and one that, despite the increasing number of people cohabiting, still appeals to many couples in love.

More practically, and despite legalities (which vary from country to country) that may cover mutual ownership of possessions after a certain period of cohabitation, some people feel it's an insecure and risky lifestyle. That, of course, causes constant debate as to whether cohabiting encourages people to view a relationship as "temporary," with the ability for either partner to walk away from it easily with little restriction, legal or otherwise. And we all have heard the sad stories of hearts (and finances) broken when such arrangements fall apart. The lifestyle may not be suitable, therefore, for anyone who cannot live with insecurity and who requires more than an emotional and physical bond for their happiness.

But for later daters, cohabitation can possibly be the perfect way to spend this time of their life — in a situation where all but the legal papers make it marital.

Again, as I have stated in previous chapters, it's wise for those who wish to retain control of their finances and possessions to have a written, legal contract drawn up when moving in together, no matter what age group. However, I gather from lawyers that few are willing to do that, perhaps convinced that the relationship will last forever or, given the chance of closeness, may develop into marriage. Perhaps, above all, many do not want to undermine something that has just begun by appearing mercenary. But if the relationship should end, they sadly always wish they had followed such advice.

Much of the advice for cohabiting applies equally to marriage, with a particular emphasis on ensuring that finances and possessions are dealt with beforehand with a prenuptial agreement. Later daters, in particular, should also make sure that they have a legal will that gets updated if they are considering marriage. This is especially essential if they have children and grandchildren they want to look after financially after they die. It's also essential that the will gets updated from time to time, particularly after a divorce or a partner's passing.

Friends with benefits

For some later daters, the thought of living together, cohabiting, getting married, or even sharing each other's homes is enough to make them break out in hives. But it doesn't mean that everything below the waist has stopped working or wanting attention. Many later daters still want sexual contact but don't want a regular relationship. It's a result of the contemporary, casual view of sexual contact and release that you don't necessarily have to have a close relationship with someone you have sex with.

Most later daters are not interested in one-night stands with strangers, which carry a high personal and health risk, so having a close friend who is comfortable with the idea of being a "sex buddy," without demanding anything more, can be appealing. You both get what you want with no strings attached. There may be physical passion but no emotional connection beyond that.

The drawbacks are obvious. Many women cannot help but bond with the person they have sex with, so it can be painful if that happens when the partner has no intention of reciprocating those feelings. Also, some later daters feel the disconnect is too hard to handle if there isn't some sort of emotional synchronization between them, resulting in them feeling they've become a mere "booty call."

Whereas the friends-with-benefits arrangement might work for some men and women weary of emotional involvement, in my experience, the more mature the dater, the more they want mutual emotional and physical bonding in a relationship, sexual or not. In other words — they want love.

The Final Say

With the increasing numbers of single female Boomers and beyond, the world of later dating is inevitably going to expand. But many women are still fearful of dipping their toe into what they see as unknown and murky waters.

Yet those who make the decision to launch themselves, find that later dating can open the door to a great adventure —a fun, often joyous, life-enhancing and refreshing learning experience at a time when it's possible you thought you knew (and had experienced) everything.

The bottom line is that dating can also lead to your finding that great partner, perhaps a soulmate, to share the rest of your life with.

Even if it doesn't happen for you, the very fact that you are actively dating means that you are still very much engaged with life, living, and, especially, love. After all, as the saying goes — you can't win if you don't play.

Later dating also means that you're an integral part of a new social revolution for single older women forging a path rarely attempted (or accepted) in the past. It's a bold, brave, pioneering movement, and you should be proud of helping lay the foundation for generations to follow.

As the author of *The Later Dater*, I feel that if this advice book helps even one 50-plus-or-older woman rediscover that spirit of being alive, find love, and rediscover the pleasure of sharing life with someone special, then writing it has been very worthwhile, and I will be delighted and satisfied.

Strength, purpose, and good luck to all women who are, or will become, later daters, and may you all find love, happiness, and joy with someone new.

Valerie Gibson

About the Author

Valerie Gibson is a well known relationships expert, writer and media personality based in Toronto, Canada.

A journalist for most of her adult life, she was, for many years, the sex and relationships columnist for a Toronto newspaper and hosted her own live advice television show *Dear Valerie*.

She has been a guest on many well known talk shows in the U.S. and Canada including Dr. Phil, Montel Williams, Maury, Prime Time Live and The Today show as well as on numerous radio shows and in documentaries.

Her previous book *Cougar: A Guide for Older Women Dating Younger Men* launched the cougar trend worldwide. Her aim was to give 40-plus women a self esteem boost by showing them they were still sexy and desirable and that dating younger was a fun and exciting option for them.

The new book, *The Later Dater*, follows her goal of helping women to be upbeat and positive about aging. Written by someone who is in the age group and who is dating herself, it encourages and helps those who are single again at 50 plus, to make the complex world of modern dating work for them and give them a fresh, new relationship start.

"I want women to enjoy the wonderful adventure of aging instead of fearing it. Meeting someone new through dating can be one option to make getting older a fulfilling and exciting time."

Valerie Gibson is currently single and living in Toronto, Canada.

Visit Valerie's website at www.valeriegibson.com

There has *never* been a better time
to be an older woman!

So many choices, options, opportunities and
freedoms previously denied to us…and now it's
possible to find another relationship,
no matter what your age.

Enjoy your exciting journey to find happiness again!

You deserve it!

Valerie